McGraw-Hill's
400 ESSENTIAL
SAT WORDS

McGraw-Hill's
400 ESSENTIAL
SAT WORDS

Denise Pivarnik-Nova

McGRAW-HILL

New York | Chicago | San Francisco | Lisbon
London | Madrid | Mexico City | Milan | New Delhi
San Juan | Seoul | Singapore | Sydney | Toronto

1 2 3 4 5 6 7 8 9 0   DOC/DOC   0 9 8 7 6 5 4

ISBN 0-07-143494-1

This publication is designed to provide accurate and authoritative information in regard to the subject matter covered. It is sold with the understanding that neither the author nor the publisher is engaged in rendering legal, accounting, or other professional service. If legal advice or other expert assistance is required, the services of a competent professional person should be sought. —*From a declaration of principles jointly adopted by a committee of the American Bar Association and a committee of publishers*

McGraw-Hill books are available at special discounts to use as premiums and sales promotions, or for use in corporate training programs. For more information, please write to the Director of Special Sales, Professional Publishing, McGraw-Hill, Two Penn Plaza, New York, NY 10121-2298. Or contact your local bookstore.

 This book is printed on recycled, acid-free paper containing a minimum of 50% recycled de-inked paper.

SECTION I

SECTION II

SECTION III

SECTION IV

SECTION I

Introduction

So, you are studying for the New SAT I. Good for you. This book will introduce you to a lot of words that you are likely to find on the SAT I. The New SAT I no longer has a separate Verbal section as it did in the past. Instead, the vocabulary has become part of the Reading Comprehension section. In fact, there are no longer any analogies, which are vocabulary questions that students have struggled with for years. Instead, the vocabulary you will be asked about is incorporated into reading passages and sentence completions. You will be expected to know the correct words to use based on their context. That's why you have this book. Not only will it provide you with words and their meanings, but each section is also followed by sentence completion and words-in-context stories for you to complete. In addition, you will find three short, comprehensive exercises that will ask you to recall words from several sections at once. The SAT I is not an easy test, but, with some studying and effort on your part, you can do well. So let's begin.

SAT I
Test-Taking Tips

WHEN WRONG INFORMATION IS THE RIGHT ANSWER

Sometimes in multiple-choice test situations you are asked a question that reads something like, "All the following items are present except . . . ." Then you have to figure out which of the five responses you are given is *not* present in whatever you are looking at.

Questions like this are sometimes tricky. For your entire school life you have been asked to find the right answer, which usually means identifying the correct piece of information. Now, suddenly, you are being asked to identify that which is incorrect, and this incorrect information is the right answer! That's tough.

Also, these questions can be time-consuming. You are no longer looking for just one piece of information to answer the question. Instead, you must methodically identify the four items that are true (or present) before you discover the one that is not correct.

The best way to do well on these questions is to practice, practice, practice. In addition, it is helpful if you glance at the five choices and again skim the information that is under consideration, ticking them off one by one as you discover them.

Admittedly this type of multiple-choice question does require some mental gymnastics on your part. After you have taken many SAT practice exams, you will be prepared for such questions, and you'll find that they don't take you nearly as long as they did before you knew what to expect.

TEST TIPS FOR THE NEW SAT I

The new SAT no longer has a section designated "Verbal." Instead the English part of the test is now separated into two sections: Writing and Critical Reading.

The Writing section includes *identifying sentence errors, improving sentences,* and *improving paragraphs* as well as a 25-minute essay that you will write based upon a prompt you will be given.

The Critical Reading section will contain *reading passages* and *questions,* along with *sentence completion (vocabulary)* questions similar to those on the SAT in the past. Reading passages will include nonfiction selections from humanities, social studies, and natural sciences, as well fiction. In addition, the new SAT will include new shorter reading passages, with paragraphs about 100 words long, followed by one or two questions similar to the longer reading passages. There may also be a pair of paragraphs, about 200 words long, with four questions based on the two passages and the relationship between the passages.

TEST TIPS FOR THE NEW SAT I

PREFIXES

Prefixes are a group of letters (known as *affixes*) placed before a word that affect its meaning. For example, take the word *able,* meaning competent or adept. When you put the prefix *un-* before it, the word becomes *unable,* meaning not able or not capable. When you put the prefix *dis-* before it, the word becomes *disable,* which means to render inoperable, for example, a car with a blown engine is a *disabled* vehicle.

There are hundreds of prefixes, and you don't have to know them all. But some you should recognize as signals about the meanings of words.

The prefixes *ir-, il-, im-, in-, un-,* and *dis-* all have to do with a negative or an opposite. The prefixes *co-, con-,* and *com-* mean *with* or in *conjunction with*. Other prefixes include *auto-, dis-, bi-, tri-, anti-,* and *inter-*.

Once you become aware of prefixes, and remember the most common ones, you will have one more clue about new words you encounter. Perhaps you don't exactly know the meaning of the word *discompose,* but you do know that if a person is composed, he or she has his act together. Therefore, *discomposed* means that the person is agitated or upset, or is in a tizzy about something.

··

TEST-TAKING TIPS FOR THE NEW SAT I
··

SUFFIXES

Suffixes are word endings that, when affixed to a word, can change the meaning and part of speech of the original word. Endings such as *-ness* and *-ability* can change an adjective into a noun. For example, consider the adjective *noble.* When you add the suffix *-ness,* you turn it into the noun *nobleness,* which means decency and righteousness. If you add the suffix *-abilty,* then you have created the noun *nobility,* which means graciousness and sometimes means the aristocracy, or the upper class.

On the other hand, the suffix *-ly* almost always indicates the adverb form of a word: *Nobly* means graciously or with honor. Adverbs almost always answer the question *how, when, why, to what extent, how often,* or *how much.* In other words, "The young princess behaved *nobly* when she visited the orphanage" tells us *how* she behaved.

Another common suffix is *-ology,* which means *the study of.* For instance, *biology* is the study of bios or life forms, and *endocrinology* is the study of the endocrine system.

Just as with prefixes, you need to become familiar with the most common suffixes. Although a suffix probably won't tell you what a word means, it will help you recognize how the word is being used. Sometimes knowing how a word is used is a critical step in figuring out its meaning.

TEST TIPS FOR THE NEW SAT I

You don't ever want to "blind guess" on the SATs. If you cannot eliminate at least two responses on a multiple-choice question, you should never make a guess at the answer. On the SAT your score is determined by the number of responses you give correctly. A blank response is neutral; an incorrect response results in .25 (1/4) point being subtracted from your score.

In other words, if you have ten questions and you leave four blank, you have a +6 score. If you have the same ten questions, but the four are incorrect, you have a +5 score. You need to have a "sense" of a response being correct and several options being incorrect before you take a guess and fill in an answer on the SAT.

TEST TIPS FOR THE NEW SAT I

Recognizing unfamiliar vocabulary words as nouns, verbs, adjectives, and adverbs is sometimes beneficial when you are trying to figure out which word or word pair is best for the sentence completion questions.

Nouns name a person, place, or thing. To check if a word is in its noun form, you should be able to put *a, an,* or *the* in front of it. For example, take the word *defiance.* The *defiance* of the prisoner tried the patience of his lawyer.

Verbs are words that show action or state of existence. In the Vocabulary section of the SAT I, verbs will be of the action type, even if they are mental action such as *to think* or *to study.* The prisoner *defied* the rules of the prison, so he lost all his privileges.

Adjectives modify nouns or pronouns. They help create a descriptive picture. The *defiant* prisoner had to be placed in solitary confinement because he would not follow the prison rules.

Adverbs modify verbs, adjectives, or other adverbs. They very often end in *-ly.* The prisoner *defiantly* refused to speak to his lawyer. (*Defiantly* modifies the verb; that is, it shows *how* he refused.) The *defiantly* rude prisoner had to find a new defense lawyer. (*Defiantly* modifies the adjective *rude;* it explains *how* he was rude.)

SECTION II

Unit 1 Reality or Illusion ►actuality, applicable, authenticity, bona fide, categorical, defensible, factual, genuine, invulnerable, legitimacy, materiality, pragmatic, real McCoy, tangible, tenable, truism, unassailable, valid, veracity, veritable ►aberration, artifice, chimera, deceptive, ephemeral, erroneous, evanescent, fallacy, fantasy, fleeting, hallucination, illusion, imaginative, imprecise, inaccurate, mirage, phantasm, semblance, short-lived, transient, whimsy **11**

Unit 2 How Often? ►contingent, episodic, incidental, intermittent, interrupt, oscillate, periodic, recurrent, spasmodic, sporadic, transitory, vacillate ►chronic, coherent, habitual, incessant, indefatigable, insistent, inveterate, perpetual, persevering, persistent, resistant, unremitting **29**

Unit 3 In Order of Importance ►extraneous, immaterial, impalpable, incidental, inconsequential, insubstantial, irrelevant, jot, modicum, nonessential, subordinate, subsidiary, whit ►abstruse, considerable, estimable, intense, momentous, noteworthy, poignant, portend, portentous, profound, rarefied, significant, substantial **43**

Unit 4 Crystal Clear and Sure or Shadowy, Uncertain, and Disturbed ►apparent, arrant, clarity, conspicuous, discernible, distinct, evident, intelligibility, limpid, lucidity, manifest, obvious, ostensibly, palpable, patently, pellucid, perceptible, perspicacity, ubiquitous ►abash, addle, anarchy, baffle, bamboozle, bedlam, bewilderment, confounded, derangement, din, discombobulated, disconcerted, moil, muddle, perplexed, pother, welter **57**

Reality or Illusion

I s the information we receive from television advertisements real and true or is it *fantasies* spun by the big business of advertising? We are constantly bombarded with information that we should carefully screen and categorize according to its *validity* or *inaccuracy*. Our language offers us a great many words to help us distinguish between *whimsy* and *bona fide truisms*.

actuality	genuine	tenable
applicable	invulnerable	truism
authenticity	legitimacy	unassailable
bona fide	materiality	valid
categorical	pragmatic	veracity
defensible	real McCoy	veritable
factual	tangible	

....

aberration	fallacy	inaccurate
artifice	fantasy	mirage
chimera	fleeting	phantasm
deceptive	hallucination	semblance
ephemeral	illusion	short-lived
erroneous	imaginative	transient
evanescent	imprecise	whimsy

► **actuality**
noun

The state of being actual or real; truly existing.

On Halloween the children were so taken by the costumes that they had a difficult time distinguishing between *actuality* and pretend.

Adjective: **actual**

► **applicable**
adjective

Readily usable; practical.

Lorena was not sure that her ideas were *applicable* to the problem, but she offered them, nevertheless.

Noun: **applicability**

► **authenticity**
noun

The quality or condition of being authentic, trustworthy, or genuine.

Before paying the high price for the Picasso painting, the art dealer had to check the *authenticity* of the work.

Adjective: **authentic**
Adverb: **authentically**

► **bona fide**
adjective

• Authentic and genuine. authenticity.

Among all the knockoffs in the shoe store, I found an inexpensive pair of *bona fide* Dr. Martens.

• Made and carried out in good faith.

The offer on the farmhouse was a *bona fide* agreement; the seller and buyer shook hands to secure the deal.

► **categorical**
adjective

- Without exception; absolute and explicit.

Nobody in the room doubted that Samuel was the *categorical* winner of the Lincoln-Douglas debate.

- Of or relating to categories or arrangement or order.

Sammy was so left-brained, logical, and sequential that no one was surprised when she put all her information in precise, *categorical* order.

► **defensible**
adjective

Justifiable for accuracy.

Maria had a *defensible* position: There was no doubt that she would win the debate.

Noun: **defensibility, defensibleness**
Adverb: **defensibly**

► **factual**
adjective

Of the nature of fact; real.

Even though the book was a work of fiction, it was full of *factual* information about that historical era.

Noun: **factuality**
Adverb: **factually**

► **genuine**
adjective

Not counterfeit, but authentic; honest and real; free from hypocrisy or dishonesty; sincere.

My uncle gave me a *genuine* two-dollar bill for my birthday.

Noun: **genuineness**
Adverb: **genuinely**

► **invulnerable**
adjective

Impossible to damage or enter; not able to alter the reality.

The front door seemed *invulnerable;* it was made of steel, and it sported seven strong locks as well.

Adverb: **invulnerably**
Noun: **invulnerability**

► **legitimacy**
noun

The quality of being legitimate—authentic, genuine, and according to the law.

The painting was suspect, so the *legitimacy* of its authenticity was questionable.

Adverb: **legitimately**
Adjective: **legitimate**

► **materiality**
noun

• The state of being material.

Esther was so intent upon possessing things that her friends started questioning her focus on *materiality*.

• Being of real or substantive quality.

In *Macbeth*, Banquo's ghost appears to Macbeth with such *materiality* that he is overwhelmed by guilt over Banquo's murder.

Adjective: **material**
Adverb: **materially**

► **pragmatic**
adjective

Dealing with facts, reality, and actual occurrences.

Aaron's insubstantial reasons were not *pragmatic,* so consequently no one believed him.

Adverb: **pragmatically**
Noun: **pragmatism**

► **real McCoy**
noun

An authentic thing or quality; something that is not an imitation or a substitute.

The real thing.

The classic 1964 Ford Mustang was the *real McCoy;* not only had it not had any body work done on it, but it had never been repainted.

► **tangible**
adjective

Possible to touch; possible to be treated as fact; real or concrete.

Carlos's fantasy became *tangible* when Angie, the girl of his dreams, agreed to go out with him.

Noun: **tangibility**
Adverb: **tangibly**

► **tenable**
adjective

Capable of being maintained; able to be maintained because of genuineness.

The team's successful season was barely *tenable* because of the girls' growing apathy toward attending practice.

Adverb: **tenably**

▶ **truism**
noun

Self-evident truth, actuality, and reality.

The rumor about a possible scandal became a *truism* once the facts were released to the public.

▶ **unassailable**
adjective

Undeniable, actual, and authentic.

The *unassailable* truth came out when Marla's little brother realized that their parents were really the Tooth Fairy.

Noun: **unassailability**
Adverb: **unassailably**

▶ **valid**
adjective

Real, authentic, correct; sound and well-grounded.

Benny Lee was able to draw a *valid* conclusion only after he had discovered all the facts.

Noun: **validity**
Adverb: **validly**

▶ **veracity**
noun

Adherence to truth, reality, accuracy, and precision.

The teacher confirmed the *veracity* of the student's late pass by checking with the teacher who supposedly wrote the pass.

▶ **veritable**
adjective

Being truly so-called; real or genuine.

A *veritable* stranger was kind enough to give Suzanne enough money to use the phone so she could call home.

Adverb: **veritably**

► **aberration**
noun

A defect or departure from the normal; deviation or imperfection.

My mother was not sure whether her occasionally seeing her dead great grandmother was real or an *aberration.*

Adjective: **aberrant**

► **artifice**
noun

Pretense, deception, or ruse.

The young woman was about 90 percent *artifice* and only 10 percent authentic.

Adjective: **artificial**
Adverb: **artificially**

► **chimera**
noun

• A fanciful mental illusion or fabrication.

The new history teacher seemed to be a *chimera*—one-half despot and one-half concerned mentor.

• An organism, organ, or part consisting of two or more tissues of different genetic composition.

The *chimera* of Greek mythology was a fire-breathing she monster who had a lion's head, a goat's body, and a snake's tail.

► **deceptive**
adjective

Tending to deceive, betray, or fool; unauthentic and untrue.

The burglar was *deceptive* because he left the front door unlocked, even though he entered and left the house from the rear.

Adverb: **deceptively**
Noun: **deception**

► **ephemeral**
adjective

Not real or authentic for any length of time; fleeting.

The thrill of tearing down a hill on a sled is *ephemeral* because soon you have to get off the sled and climb to the top of the hill again.

► **erroneous**
adjective

Mistaken and untrue.

Erroneous information led the police force to pursue the wrong suspect.

Noun: **erroneousness**
Adverb: **erroneously**

► **evanescent**
adjective

To disappear of likely to disappear.

Vanishing or likely to vanish; without much substance.

One's dreams are often *evanescent,* because, soon after waking, most people forget the details.

Noun: **evanescence**
Verb: **evanesce**

► **fallacy**
noun

• A false notion.

It is a *fallacy* to think black cats bring bad luck.

• A rhetorical flaw in an argument.

There was such a glaring *fallacy* in the lawyer's argument that it was no surprise that he lost the case.

• An untruth.

Some pessimists believe that true love is a *fallacy*; it just doesn't exist.

Adjective: **fallacious**

► **fantasy**
noun

A creation of the imagination; an imagined event; a dream.

Tolkien is the author who introduced the reading public to a genre of fiction known as *fantasy* novels.

Adjective: **fantastic, fantastical**
Verb: **fantasize**

► **fleeting**
adjective

Passing quickly; ephemeral.

We caught a *fleeting* glimpse at the squirrel as it scampered away from the bird feeder.

Adverb: **fleetingly**

► **hallucination**
noun

• A false or mistaken idea; a delusion.

After my grandfather's death, my grandmother experienced some strong *hallucinations* in which her late husband talked to her.

• A multisensory experience with no external stimulus, often drug-induced.

While coming out of the anesthetic after my surgery, I kept having very strange *hallucinations.*

Adjective: **hallucinatory**
Verb: **hallucinate**

► **illusion**
noun

An erroneous perception of reality; a fantastical plan.

Chaltu had a strong *illusion* about the possibility of someone following her.

Adjective: **illusionary**

► **imaginative**
adjective

Having a lively, creative mind; creating fantastic dreams.

imaginary
adjective

Not real, from the imagination.

It is not unusual for a child, especially an only child, to be very *imaginative* and to create an *imaginary* friend.

Adverb: **imaginatively**
Verb: **imagine**

► **imprecise**
adjective

Not precise; not exact or sure.

Since Mallory's answer was rather *imprecise,* Mathew's response sounded intelligent and specific by comparison.

Noun: **imprecision**
Adverb: **imprecisely**

► **inaccurate**
adjective

Mistaken or incorrect; not accurate.

Abraham stood by his beliefs and principles whether they were *inaccurate* or exact.

Noun: **inaccuracy**
Adverb: **inaccurately**

► **mirage**
noun

• Something that is illusory or insubstantial.

Thomas always visualized the *mirage* of a six-figure income.

• An optical phenomenon that creates the illusion of water.

A typical *mirage* is a green and lush oasis in the middle of a desert.

► **phantasm**
noun

Something apparently seen but without any true physical presence; an illusion of the brain; a ghost or spirit.

Despite the reaction from others, Paula wasn't sure if she was experiencing a real explanation for what had happened, or just a *phantasm* of her imagination.

Adjective: **phantasmal**

► **semblance**
noun

Outward appearance; a representation or a copy of something else.

Although the students were very excited, the principal was able to get them into some *semblance* of order.

Adjective: **semblable**

► **short-lived**
adjective

Living or lasting only a short while; fleeting.

The team's 2-point lead was *short-lived*, for soon the other team got two baskets in a row.

► **transient**
adjective, noun

Adjective: Passing in time; remaining or existing only briefly.

Noun: One who passes through without permanent bonds.

When I was growing up, my family led a *transient* life.

When I was growing up I was a *transient,* because my father was in the U.S. Air Force; we moved to a new place every two or three years.

The *transient* moved from one warm doorway to another until he got a feel for the new town.

Adverb: **transiently**

The homeless person lived *transiently,* one night at a shelter and other nights flopping with a friend.

► **whimsy**
noun

A whim or an odd or fanciful idea; sometimes a quaint or unorthodox idea.

Acting upon mere *whimsy,* Francis went to talk to the assistant principal, and his plans were, surprisingly, approved.

Adjective: **whimsical**
Adverb: **whimsically**

Sentence Completion

Circle the word pair that best completes the meaning of the sentence.

1. The accused man's lawyer had to create a _____ case that would be _____ to the attack of the prosecuting attorney.

   A. defensible/invulnerable
   B. categorical/pragmatic
   C. factual/ephemeral
   D. valid/erroneous
   E. genuine/tenable

2. My uncle led a very _____ life; he would come and go, based solely on whatever _____ controlled him at that time.

   A. genuine/materiality
   B. categorical/chimera
   C. transient/whimsy
   D. unassailable/aberration
   E. defensible/truism

3. The oasis in the desert was just a _____, only a _____, or an illusion of green on the endless sand and under the unforgiving sun.

   A. whimsy/short-lived
   B. mirage/phantasm
   C. legitimacy/real McCoy
   D. aberration/fallacy
   E. chimera/actuality

4. Flora made a(n) _____ assumption about her teacher; after a couple months she realized he was _____ interested in his students above everything else.

   A. applicable/pragmatically
   B. actual/categorically
   C. erroneous/genuinely
   D. invulnerable/whimsically
   E. whimsical/transiently

5. The coach's favor with the public was _____; once the team started losing games, his fans' belief in him was only _____—here today and gone tomorrow.

   A. semblance/authentic
   B. transient/fleeting
   C. hallucinatory/imprecise
   D. inaccurate/legitimate
   E. invulnerable/phantasmal

Quick Matching

Write the letter of the definition shown in the right column next to the word that matches it in the left column.

_____1. categorical	A. capable of being maintained
_____2. materiality	B. justifiable accuracy
_____3. veracity	C. self-evident, actually
_____4. tenable	D. a reality of substance
_____5. defensible	E. absolute, explicit, and without exception

Complete the Story

Using these words selected from this unit, fill in the blanks to complete the story.

categorical	unassailable
genuine	pragmatic
fleeting	fallacious
legitimate	deceptive
artifice	tangible
tenable	chimera
evanescent	mirage
legitimacy	legitimate
actuality	bona fide
whimsy	ephemeral
imaginative	valid
veracity	

The art and _____ of the advertisement business is a _____ study of _____ and _____ versus the _____ and the _____. Advertising itself is a _____, a union of two opposites. Nowhere else in our lives are so many promises offered to us than through the world of ads. We are not supposed to consider how _____ and without substance these promises really are. Instead, consumers are supposed to accept what they are told as _____ information, _____ truths, and _____ hopes based upon _____ facts.

In reality, advertising is the business of building for us a supposedly _____ world in which we are promised _____ _____ improvements to our lives, to our families, and to all that we consider important. If we experience momentary, _____ doubts about a product's assurances, we quickly shift our minds and pretend that it was simply an _____ perception or even a _____ that never existed as a real, _____ thought. Advertisers do not want their viewing public to be _____. They convince us of the _____ of their claims; they offer us _____, short-lived promises, convincing us with _____ arguments and gentle persuasion. Consumers, unfortunately, are often immune to such ploys, and they rush right out to their latest, have-to-have _____.

ANSWERS

Sentence completion: 1-A, 2-C, 3-B, 4-C, 5-B.

Quick matching: 1-E, 2-D, 3-B, 4-A, 5-C.

Complete the story: artifice, categorical, actuality, veracity, imaginative, deceptive, chimera, evanescent, valid, unassailable, tenable, tangible, genuine, bona fide, fleeting, erroneous, mirage, legitimate, pragmatic, legitimacy, ephemeral, fallacious, whimsy.

How Often?

Have you ever had to fill out a survey that asked you to rate the frequency with which you do one thing or another? For instance, a survey about television viewing habits might ask if the viewer watches sports events on television *often, occasionally, once in a while, rarely,* or *never.* You know the sort of survey. Following is a bunch of words that most of the survey writers have probably never heard of. Maybe you can put them together to create your own frequency survey. There's no doubt that you could do a better job than most of the professional survey makers, who seem limited in their word choices.

contingent	interrupt	spasmodic
episodic	oscillate	sporadic
incidental	periodic	transitory
intermittent	recurrent	vacillate

• •

chronic	indefatigable	persevering
coherent	insistent	persistent
habitual	inveterate	resistant
incessant	perpetual	unremitting

► **contingent**
adjective

• Liable to occur but not with certainty; possible.

Today's weather forecast includes a *contingent* chance of showers by evening.

• Dependent on conditions or occurrences not yet established.

My cousin is a *contingent* worker; she works for a temporary employment agency.

Noun: **contingency**

► **episodic**
adjective

Relating to or happening in episodes.

The made-for-television movie was *episodic;* that is, it was broadcast in sections rather than all in one night.

Adverb: **episodically**

► **incidental**
adjective

Apt to occur in a minor or unpredictable manner.

It was an *incidental* bother; only rarely did the turn signal stick while I was driving.

Adverb: **incidentally**

► **intermittent**
adjective

Stopping and starting at intervals.

The news about the disaster was *intermittent;* the network fed the public information only a little at a time.

Noun: **intermittence**
Adverb: **intermittently**

► **interrupt**
verb

To break the rhythm or continuity; to stop the momentum or continuum.

Because of the lightning, the officials had to *interrupt* the game.

Adjective: **interrupted**
Noun: **interruption**

► **oscillate**
verb

To move back and forth; to waver or doubt a decision.

It was a hot night, and the air conditioner in the house broke down. Even the fan wouldn't *oscillate.* It just sat there, not turning, just pushing the hot air out in front of it.

Noun: **oscillation**
Adjective: **oscillating**

► **periodic**
adjective

Characterized by a repeating cycle or repetition of intervals; appearing or occurring from time to time.

Her visits to her grandparents are *periodic.* Although there is no formal agreement with them, she visits nearly every other weekend.

Adverb: **periodically**

► **recurrent**
adjective

Occurring repeatedly.

Martha kept having a *recurrent* dream; night after night she had the same nightmare.

Adverb: **recurrently**
Noun: **recurrence**

► **spasmodic**
adjective

• Having the characteristic of a spasm or convulsion.

The medication caused the patient to experience *spasmodic* episodes.

• Happening intermittently; from time to time.

The *spasmodic* sound of fireworks frightened the dog.

Adverb: **spasmodically**
Noun: **spasm**

► **sporadic**
adjective

Occurring at different intervals, with no set pattern.

The rain has been *sporadic* this summer, so people have to water their yards and gardens more often than in past summers.

Adverb: **sporadically**

► **transitory**
adjective

Short-lived; temporary; only passing, not permanent.

Josh was involved in yet another of his *transitory* love affairs; this was his fifth girlfriend in two months.

▶ **vacillate**
verb

To move back and forth, especially being unable to make up one's mind.

Michele *vacillated* constantly. She was so bad about making decisions that it took her three hours just to go grocery shopping.

Adjective: **vacillating**
Noun: **vacillation**

• •

▶ **chronic**
adjective

Of long duration or frequent recurrence; happening a great deal and/or often.

Bronchitis is usually characterized by a *chronic* cough that often causes the sufferer great discomfort and extreme exhaustion.

Noun: **chronicity**
Adverb: **chronically**

▶ **coherent**
adjective

Marked by an orderly, logical, consistent relationship; not broken up by distraction or intervening time or information; consistent.

The information has been *coherent.* For once the media have reported the facts as they occur, with few confusing asides.

Noun: **coherence**
Adverb: **coherently**
Verb: **cohere**

▶ **habitual**
adjective

Naturally out of habit or routine; regular and common.

Sonam was a *habitual* nail-biter during stressful times, so it was not unusual for her fingertips to bleed by the time she finished a challenging exam.

Adverb: **habitually**
Noun: **habit**

▶ **incessant**
adjective

Continuing without interruption, sometimes to an excessive degree.

The *incessant* rain was beginning to drive people stir-crazy; they were hoping for a break in the weather so they could get outside for a while.

Noun: **incessancy**
Adverb: **incessantly**

▶ **indefatigable**
adjective

Incapable of becoming tired or ceasing; not stopping or giving up.

The park ranger seemed to be *indefatigable;* long after everyone else was exhausted, he kept up his steady pace.

Adverb: **indefatigably**

▶ **insistent**
adjective

Firm in asserting a demand or an opinion; unyielding; repetitive.

The crows' *insistent* cries in the early morning made sleeping nearly impossible for anyone in the area.

Noun: **insistence**
Adverb: **insistently**
Verb: **insist**

▶ **inveterate**
adjective

Long established; habitual.

Pat was an *inveterate* fisherman. Although he was well into his 70s, he would go out on his boat whenever he had a chance.

Adverb: **inveterately**

▶ **perpetual**
adjective

Continuing or lasting for an indefinitely long or unlimited period of time.

The *perpetual* motion clock in the science building never needs winding or attention, because the earth's gravity is what keeps it going.

Adverb: **perpetually**
Verb: **perpetuate**

▶ **persevering**
adjective

To persist in or remain constant to a purpose, idea, or task; not giving up or giving in to obstacles.

Henri's *persevering* nature enabled him to graduate with honors despite having no support or encouragement from friends or family.

Noun: **perseverance**
Adverb: **perseveringly**
Verb: **persevere**

▶ **persistent**
adjective

Not letting up; continuing even to the point of being bothersome.

Nathan found that the *persistent* spam he kept getting on his computer was enough to cause him to change his Internet carrier.

Noun: **persistence**
Adverb: **persistently**
Verb: **persist**

▶ **resistant**
adjective

Not giving up or giving in; fighting against the odds.

The watch I received when I was 10 years old was so *resistant* to damage that I was still wearing it when I graduated from high school.

Noun: **resistance**
Verb: **resist**

► **unremitting**
adjective

Never slackening or getting any less or any easier; persistent.

Georgio's grudge was so ***unremitting*** that, long after he had forgotten the reason for their quarrel, he would still not talk to his cousin Arturo.

Noun: **unremittingness**
Adverb: **unremittingly**

Sentence Completion

Circle the word or word pair that best completes the meaning of the sentence.

1. The company's plans to move forward were not solid because everything was _____ upon its client's acceptance of the offer.

   A. recurrent
   B. contingent
   C. incessant
   D. coherent
   E. insistent

2. The child followed the back-and-forth playground taunts with the _____ attention of a tennis referee.

   A. inveterate
   B. intermittent
   C. interrupted
   D. oscillating
   E. spasmodic

3. The television news _____ the program _____ with information about the increasing devastation caused by the hurricane.

   A. interrupted/periodically
   B. perpetuated/persistently
   C. resisted/recurrently
   D. vacillated/chronically
   E. insisted/intermittently

4. The toddler's _____ crying finally diminished to a _____ whimper.

    A. indefatigable/inveterate
    B. spasmodic/coherent
    C. resistant/persevering
    D. incessant/intermittent
    E. chronic/perpetual

5. The guerilla attacks were _____, _____ about once a month.

    A. spasmodic/oscillating
    B. chronic/cohering
    C. incessant/interrupting
    D. sporadic/vacillating
    E. episodic/recurring

Quick Matching

Write the letter of the definition shown in the right column next to the word that matches it in the left column.

_____1. spasmodic	A. continuity being broken
_____2. persistent	B. fighting against all odds
_____3. perpetual	C. seeming to have no end in sight
_____4. resistant	D. happening from time to time
_____5. interrupted	E. continuing in a bothersome manner

Complete the Story

Using these words selected from this unit, fill in the blanks to complete the story.

resistant	indefatigable
episodic	vacillates
sporadic	insists
insistent	contingent
unremitting	consistently
persistently	oscillate

My best friends, Mack and Mike, are as opposite as two people can be. Whenever they are faced with decisions, Mack gets right on the situation, but Mike is wishy-washy and _____ undecided. Despite Mack's nagging, Mike is _____ to any resolution whatsoever. Whenever he is expected to make up his mind, he _____ between his choices and only rarely can he settle on an option. In contrast, Mack is always quick to decide and act. He _____ that he knows what he wants. He _____ bugs Mike to hurry up and make up his mind. In fact, he is such an _____ pest, so unrelenting in his urging, that he and Mike have often nearly come to blows over Mack's _____ clamor for his friend to just make up his mind.

Despite their differences, I am never torn in my affection toward either friend. Their contrasting behavior is so _____ that I can almost set my calendar by it. I've come to realize that Mike will _____ back and forth while trying to make up his mind. His responses always seem to be _____ upon one thing or another. On the other hand,

Mack is a rock; his decisiveness is _____; there is nothing haphazard or _____ in any of his actions.

In Order of Importance

W e often need to stress that one thing is more or less important or more or less significant than another. Saying that the movie we just saw was *okay* or that a homework assignment is *important* or that getting an increase in allowance is *really, really important* doesn't give us the distinction that we want. Below you will find words that will help you refer to the unimportant and words that will help you identify the really important.

extraneous	insubstantial	subordinate
immaterial	irrelevant	subsidiary
impalpable	jot	whit
incidental	modicum	
inconsequential	nonessential	

. . . .

abstruse	noteworthy	rarefied
considerable	poignant	significant
estimable	portend	substantial
intense	portentous	
momentous	profound	

► **extraneous**
adjective

- Having no vital importance.

Because we already had enough volunteers for the job, Charles's presence was *extraneous.*

- Coming from the outside; not innate.

When developing a successful argument, you want to stick to the facts and avoid *extraneous* bits of information.

Adverb: **extraneously**

► **immaterial**
adjective

- Of no importance; beside the point.

The piece of information that Sonya offered was *immaterial* to the solution.

- Having no material substance.

Those who talk about angels have trouble explaining their *immaterial* form.

Adverb: **immaterially**

► **impalpable**
adjective

Not able to be grasped, held, or understood.

For many who struggle with mathematics, the concept of negative numbers is as *impalpable* as trying to distinguish the individual grains that make up talcum powder.

Adverb: **impalpably**
Noun: **impalpability**

► **incidental**
adjective

Having little or no importance or impact.

The earthquake was so mild that most people in San Francisco considered it of *incidental* importance.

Adverb: **incidentally**
Noun: **incident**

► **inconsequential** • Lacking importance.
adjective

Because the law was revoked, the argument became *inconsequential* and the protestors returned home.

• Not following from premises or evidence; illogical.

Because of several logical fallacies in the argument, the debater's conclusion became *inconsequential.*

Adverb: **inconsequentially**

► **insubstantial** • Negligible in size, importance, or strength.
adjective • Delicate; flimsy; without substance.

Because Jason had not yet experienced his adolescent growth spurt, he was too *insubstantial* to play football for his junior high school.

Noun: **insubstantiality**

► **irrelevant**
adjective

Unrelated to the matter being considered.

Because Jose had little experience in the art of social conversation, he frequently made *irrelevant,* sometimes absurd, statements that would often bring the conversation to a standstill.

Adverb: **irrelevantly**
Noun: **irrelevance**

► **jot**
noun, verb

Noun: A very small bit; an iota; something of little importance.

The teacher did not care a *jot* about the student's hundredth excuse for being late.

Verb: To make a quick note; to write down a few things.

Whenever Stephen King has a brainstorm for another story, he *jots* down his thoughts so that he won't forget them.

► **modicum**
noun

A small, very modest, or token amount.

The least we should do is give the speaker a *modicum* of attention, even though she is boring us to tears.

► **nonessential**
adjective

Not essential; of little or trivial importance.

Often, when you research something on the Internet, you discover a lot of *nonessential* information before you find what's really important to your quest.

► **subordinate**
adjective, noun

Adjective: Inferior in position to another.

As a new private in the U.S. Army, Patrick was in a *subordinate* position to everyone else.

Noun: The position of inferiority.

The rank of private is the rank of a *subordinate* because it is the lowest rank in the army.

Adverb: **subordinately**
Noun: **subordination**

► **subsidiary**
adjective, noun

Adjective: Serving or augmenting another; of secondary importance.

That additional information is *subsidiary* to the specific facts of the case.

Noun: That which is in the service or augmentation of something larger.

The kiosk on the ground level of the mall is a *subsidiary* to the department store on the second level.

► **whit**
noun

The least bit; just an iota.

The child's blatant misbehavior made it clear that he did not give a *whit* about the consequences of what he was doing.

•••

► **abstruse**
adjective

Not clear; ambiguous or uncertain; sometimes highbrow and totally beyond the norm.

The witness gave such an unimaginable and *abstruse* description of what he saw that the jury found him totally unconvincing.

Adverb: **abstrusely**

► **considerable**
adjective

In a large or impressive amount or significance.

The evidence of the crime was so *considerable* that most spectators expected the jury to quickly bring back a guilty verdict.

Adverb: **considerably**

► **estimable**
adjective

• Capable of being estimated.

The *estimable* value of the dead widow's fortune was well over $1 million.

• Of considerable importance, influence, or esteem.

The homecoming queen was of such *estimable* importance to the homecoming pageant that everyone wanted to be noticed by her.

Noun: **estimation**
Adverb: **estimably**

► **intense**
adjective

- Of extreme degree, characteristics, strength, or effort.

The fire was too *intense* for the firefighters to remain in the building.

- Tending to feel deeply or profoundly.

Her mourning for her lost child became so *intense* that she needed to be sedated.

Noun: **intensity**
Adverb: **intensely**

► **momentous**
adjective

Significant and meaningful; sometimes even historically important.

The quarterback made a *momentous* decision when he opted to pass the ball, which led to Notre Dame winning the championship.

Adverb: **momentously**
Noun: **moment**

► **noteworthy**
adjective

Something worth noting or paying attention to; significant; meaningful.

It was a *noteworthy* occasion when the governor of the state spoke at her daughter's high school graduation.

Noun: **noteworthiness**

► **poignant**
adjective

Important; moving; often emotionally significant.

After the 9/11 tragedy, the ceremony to honor the fallen victims, televised from the National Cathedral in Washington, D.C., was clearly a *poignant* experience for all who were involved.

Adverb: **poignantly**
Noun: **poignance**

► **portend**
verb

To foresee and/or foretell; to have an inclination about the future.

The witches in *Macbeth* **portend** that Macbeth will become king; little did he know how dearly he would pay for their prediction.

► **portentous**
adjective

Significant, usually in a threatening or ominous way; filled with heavy misgiving.

The sky looked *portentous* with its unusual brownish green aura, and soon we heard the sound of the tornado sirens.

Adverb: **portentously**
Noun: **portent**

► **profound**
adjective

Weighty; insightful; intense; full of meaning or significance.

People who look for fun predictions about their future when they open Chinese fortune cookies are often disappointed when they get *profound* statements about life instead.

Adverb: **profoundly**
Noun: **profoundly**

▶ **rarefied**
adjective

Belonging to a select or even lofty group; elevated in character; esoteric.

My uncle was pledged to a fraternity so *rarefied* that all members had to have at least a 170 IQ in order to belong.

Noun: **rarefaction**

▶ **significant**
adjective

Of considerable importance or weighty concern.

We could tell that our summons to the principal's office was *significant* because of Mr. Lewiston's formality when we entered the room.

Adverb: **significantly**
Noun: **significance**

▶ **substantial**
adjective

Ample; considerable; sizable; of substance; sometimes even weighty or large in size.

The crowds that gathered for the protest were *substantial,* so the local police had to call on support from a neighboring jurisdiction to help with crowd control.

Adverb: **substantially**
Noun: **substantiation**

Sentence Completion

Circle the word or word pair that best completes the meaning of the sentence.

1. During the funeral, emotions became _____; there wasn't a dry eye in the church.

   A. subordinate
   B. rarefied
   C. intense
   D. considerable
   E. portentous

2. The prosecutor's case fell apart after the police questioned all the witnesses and found their testimony to be not only contradictory but also _____.

   A. rarefied
   B. significant
   C. nonessential
   D. insubstantial
   E. impalpable

3. During the Fourth of July celebration, there was such _____ noise that my mother was unable to find a _____ of quiet amidst the pandemonium.

   A. abstruse/modicum
   B. substantial/whit
   C. poignant/subordinate
   D. noteworthy/jot
   E. incidental/irrelevance

4. Since everyone had already brought a _____ amount food to the picnic, Martha's single bag of chips was _____.

   A. considerable/immaterial
   B. portentous/subordinate
   C. momentous/impalpable
   D. profound/subsidiary
   E. rarefied/insubstantial

5. The research scientist's _____ discovery of a possible cure for a unique strain of AIDS brought _____ funding to the research lab.

   A. considerable/subsidiary
   B. noteworthy/substantial
   C. incidental/profound
   D. rarefied/immaterial
   E. estimable/extraneous

Quick Matching

Write the letter of the definition shown in the right column next to the word that matches it in the left column.

_____1. extraneous

_____2. jot

_____3. rarefied

_____4. subsidiary

_____5. estimable

A. something of little or inconsequential importance

B. of no importance or significance

C. of considerable esteem or importance

D. secondary or subordinate to another

E. unusually awesome or out of the ordinary

Complete the Story

Using these words selected from this unit, fill in the blanks to complete the story.

rarefied	intense
substantial	poignant
subsidiary	profound
momentous	noteworthy
significant	jot
profound	inconsequential
extraneous	portentous
abstruse	incidental
considerable	

Mark, Jamie, and Rachelle were teamed together to do an important, _____ research project on the _____ ruin of Stonehenge. They had no idea how _____ the work would be. At first, Jamie thought that the assignment was not worth much and was _____, but then the teacher informed them that this project would be worth 25 percent of their semester grade. Suddenly, what had seemed like just one more _____ busywork activity was now a _____ part of their grade.

It did not take the three of them long to realize that no one knew a _____ about the monument or its _____ significance to early British history. As each of the team members discovered _____ pieces of information, what seemed insignificant suddenly became _____.

After they collected a _____ amount of information, they organized it into an estimable outline of facts, but some were too confusing and _____ to use, and others became _____ to the primary focus of the project. After weeks of collaboration, the _____ deadline arrived, and they turned in their project. After they breathed a sigh of relief, they looked at one another and felt good about what they had accomplished. It was a very _____ moment for them all. Rather than having _____ misgivings about their efforts, they all felt a _____ relief at a job well done.

ANSWERS

Sentence completion: 1-C, 2-D, 3-B, 4-A, 5-B.

Quick matching: 1-B, 2-A, 3-E, 4-D, 5-C.

Complete the story: significant, rarefied, intense, inconsequential, extraneous, substantial, jot, profound, incidental, noteworthy, considerable, abstruse, subsidiary, momentous, poignant, portentous, profound.

Crystal Clear and Sure or Shadowy, Uncertain, and Disturbed

Even well-ordered, organized people can be totally upset by unexpected events. Disturbed travel plans, for instance, often change the most orderly and *lucid* arrangements to *muddled bedlam*. Even *patently obvious* plans, which show *intelligibility* and *perspicacity* on the part of the planner can go awry. This is often *apparent* when *distinct* procedures are *ostensibly* altered for one reason or another. One delayed or missed flight or a missed freeway exit can perplex and bewilder even the most well-thought-out travel preparations. The next time you find yourself *disconcerted* by unexpected circumstances, here are some good words you can use to describe your plight. They can't fix the situation, but at least they will give you the vocabulary you'll need to complain about it.

apparent	intelligibility	patently
arrant	limpid	pellucid
clarity	lucidity	perceptible
conspicuous	manifest	perspicacity
discernible	obvious	ubiquitous
distinct	ostensibly	
evident	palpable	

• •

abash	bewilderment	moil
addle	confounded	muddle
anarchy	derangement	perplexed
baffle	din	pother
bamboozle	discombobulated	welter
bedlam	disconcerted	

► **apparent**
adjective

Clearly seen; visible; not obscure or confusing.

It was *apparent* that something was bothering Charles because his behavior was out of the ordinary.

Adverb: **apparently**

► **arrant**
adjective

Completely and thoroughly thus; it is what it is.

Louis's *arrant* feelings toward Celia prevented him from concentrating.

Adverb: **arrantly**

► **clarity**
noun

Clearness of thought, style, or appearance.

With sudden *clarity,* Sandra understood the calculus problem.

► **conspicuous**
adjective

Standing out; clearly exceptional or showy.

Redheaded Timothy was *conspicuous* among the dark-haired Italians in the neighborhood.

Adverb: **conspicuously**
Noun: **conspicuousness**

► **discernible**
adjective

Clearly understandable through thought or vision.

Saturn was *discernible* in the southeastern night sky, even without a telescope.

Adverb: **discernibly**
Verb: **discern**
Noun: **discernment**

► **distinct**
adjective

Clearly defined and recognizable; standing out from among its class.

Jesse's *distinct* style of dressing made it easy to pick him out of the crowd.

Adverb: **distinctly**
Adjective: **distinctive**

► **evident**
adjective

• Worthy of notice; distinguishable.

Because the reference book was so worn, it was *evident* that it was well-thumbed.

• Apparent

Because Paul's hair had such an unusual sheen, it was *evident* that he was a swimmer.

Adverb: **evidently**
Noun: **evidence**

► **intelligibility**
noun

Intellectual understanding; mental clarity.

The chimpanzee demonstrated such *intelligibility* in his responses to the scientists that it was difficult for them to remember that they were working with an animal and not a human.

Adjective: **intelligible**
Adverb: **intelligibly**

► **limpid**
adjective

Clear and clean; without blemish or confusion.

Emily's *limpid* eyes said it all; she was truly in love with Clarence.

Adverb: **limpidly**

► **lucidity**
noun

Clearness of thought; capacity to perceive the thought.

Clarence, however, lacked the *lucidity* to recognize Emily's adoration.

Adverb: **lucidly**
Adjective: **lucid**

► **manifest**
verb

To show plainly; to reveal.

He *manifested* his displeasure in his body language and tone of voice.

Adverb: **manifestly**
Adjective: **manifest**

► **obvious**
adjective

Apparent; easily seen or seen through; without subterfuge.

Laurel's *obvious* pleasure was apparent in her facial expression.

Adverb: **obviously**
Noun: **obviousness**

► **ostensibly**
adverb

Seeming to mean something or to be interpreted as such.

Although we were *ostensibly* invited because we were friends of the host, in reality, he was using our presence to enhance his political position in the community.

Adjective: **ostensible**

► **palpable**
adjective

Clear and discernible; noticeable by touch.

The unease among the group members was *palpable* as they stared at their feet and cleared their throats.

Adverb: **palpably**

► **patently**
adverb

Openly; plainly; clearly.

It was *patently* clear from the reaction of the jury that the defense attorney had the upper hand.

The lackadaisical behavior of the seniors *patently* indicated their senioritis.

Adjective: **patent**

► **pellucid**
adjective

Clear in style, manner, or appearance.

Her *pellucid* attempts to impress the young man were useless since he was more interested in watching the football game.

Adverb: **pellucidly**

► **perceptible**
adjective

Capable of being perceived by the senses or the intellect.

The change in atmospheric pressure was *perceptible* to me as soon as I felt a headache developing.

Noun: **perception**
Adverb: **perceptively**

▶ **perspicacity**
noun

Acuteness of perception and understanding.

The five-year-old's ***perspicacity*** amazed all who heard him answer the question.

Adjective: **perspicacious**
Adverb: **perspicaciously**

▶ **ubiquitous**
adjective

All over; always present and noticeable.

The new principal was ***ubiquitous*** that fall; he went out of his way to show students that he cared and that he was always around if they needed him.

Adverb: **ubiquitously**
Noun: **ubiquity**

• •

▶ **abash**
verb

To confuse or distress; to cause perplexity and uncertainty.

He ***abashed*** his opponent by unearthing a past embarrassing incident that few people knew about.

Adjective: **abashed**
Adverb: **abashedly**

▶ **addle**
verb

Cause to become unclear or confusing.

Rene ***addled*** the frail, old librarian by being rude and indifferent to the man's senior position and personal feelings.

Adjective: **addled**

► **anarchy**
noun

- Confusion and disruption; without clearness in mind or purpose.

Once the teacher left the room, all order fell apart and the students resorted to total *anarchy.*

- Government without a designated leader.

After the overthrow of the king, *anarchy* ruled throughout the country.

► **baffle**
verb

To confuse; to forestall action or understanding.

The prosecution lawyer tried to *baffle* the witness with his cleverness, but the witness was too smart and would not be dissuaded from her testimony.

Adjective: **baffled**
Noun: **bafflement**

► **bamboozle**
verb

To trick and confuse.

The wily student's attempt to *bamboozle* the counselor with double-talk did not work, and he was promptly sent back to class.

Adjective: **bamboozled**

► **bedlam**
noun

- A place of noisy uproar and confusion.

When the substitute teacher arrived, she found the classroom in a state of *bedlam* and it took her the remainder of the hour to restore order.

- An insane asylum (old-fashioned term).

In the Victorian era in England, mental patients were confined to *bedlam.*

► **bewilderment**
noun

State of being confused, perplexed, and/or disoriented.

Hansel's and Gretel's **bewilderment** was so obvious that it did not take the witch long to coerce them into her home.

Verb: **bewilder**
Adjective: **bewildered**

► **confounded**
adjective

Confused or stunned; totally perplexed.

Patricia was **confounded** by her boss's change of heart when he granted her extra vacation over the holidays so that she could visit her family in New Mexico.

Adverb: **confoundedly**
Verb: **confound**

► **derangement**
noun

Disturbance or disorderliness; maximum confusion to the point of mental instability.

There was such a **derangement** in the classroom that the teacher thought she would surely lose her mind before the end of the semester.

Adjective: **deranged**

► **din**
noun

Loud noise or confusion, usually from a crowd.

Often, indoor stadiums are poorly equipped to handle noise so that the **din** can be overwhelming for the crowds who come to view the games.

► **discombobulated**
adjective

Confused and taken off guard by circumstances.

My cousin became so *discombobulated* by the accident that her usually calm demeanor was no longer in evidence.

Verb: **discombobulate**
Noun: **discombobulation**

► **disconcerted**
adjective

Upset; confused; put off balance.

My grandmother was so *disconcerted* by the news that she was unable to speak for several minutes,

Adverb: **disconcertedly**
Verb: **disconcert**

► **moil**
noun

A situation that is confused, in a turmoil, and/or uncertain.

Patrick William found himself in such a *moil* that he thought he would never be able to save himself.

► **muddle**
verb

To think, act, or proceed in a confused or aimless manner.

Not clear about exactly what was expected of him on the new job, Giorgio *muddled* along until somebody gave him specific directions.

Adjective: **muddled**

▶ **perplexed**
adjective

Confused, or bewildered.

Wilma was ***perplexed*** by the disappearance of her glasses and didn't realize they were on the top of her head.

Verb: **perplex**
Noun: **perplexity**

▶ **pother**
noun

A commotion or a disturbance; a state of nervous activity.

My little sister was in such a ***pother*** about her impending piano recital that I was concerned that she would forget how to play her piece.

▶ **welter**
noun

A confused mass; a jumble; total disorganization and perplexity.

The poorly organized field trip was a ***welter*** of miscommunication and disgruntled children.

Sentence Completion

Circle the word or word pair that best completes the meaning of the sentence.

1. Visibility was so poor that the headlights of the oncoming car were barely _____ in the fog.

   A. conspicuous
   B. arrant
   C. discernible
   D. obvious
   E. manifest

2. Martha's wild story was so _____ a lie that I couldn't believe the teacher was falling for it.

   A. ostensibly
   B. patently
   C. intelligibly
   D. limpidly
   E. palpably

3. Drew's _____ was so _____ that the calculus teacher went over the problem once again.

   A. lucidity/evident
   B. clarity/manifest
   C. bafflement/addled
   D. perplexity/apparent
   E. derangement/discombobulated

4. Ryan's messy desk was such a _____ of papers and files that it was _____ he would never find the sheet of figures he was looking for.

A. din/confounded
B. bewilderment/discernible
C. intelligibility/palpable
D. muddle/obvious
E. pother/conspicuous

5. There was such a _____ in the classroom that the substitute teacher became totally _____.

A. din/discombobulated
B. derangement/ostensive
C. bedlam/limpid
D. clarity/intelligible
E. bafflement/confounded

Quick Matching

Write the letter of the definition shown in the right column next to the word that matches it in the left column.

_____1. disconcerted	A.	clearly defined and recognizable
_____2. muddled	B.	confused and causing uncertainty and embarrassment
_____3. abashed	C.	standing out from the rest
_____4. conspicuous	D.	seeming to act aimlessly, without reason
_____5. distinct	E.	confused and thrown off balance mentally

Complete the Story

Using these words selected from this unit, fill in the blanks to complete the story.

bewilderment	perplexing
perceptible	discernible
muddled	evidently
apparent	baffle
perspicacity	lucidity
evidence	confounded
moil	

Mystery stories have _____ gained a conspicuous place in the hearts of reading or viewing audiences. Some mysteries have clearly _____ story lines and easily _____ clues; they do not _____ the audience with _____ plots or unusual characters. In contrast, some mysteries are so un_____ that the viewer/reader is uncertain of the truth until the last moment. These plots are often _____ with unusual twists, and the action is in such a _____ that one finds it difficult to figure out what is going on.

Main characters in mysteries are a big part of the stories' success. Sometimes these are unique personalities, such as the old television cop Columbo or Agatha Christie's Hercule Poirot. These characters often act _____ and confused about what is going on, while actually they are cleverly getting to the bottom of the problem. Their supposed _____ is their strongest weapon. Other mystery solvers, such as Sherlock Holmes, are known for their fine intelligence and steel-trap memories. No _____ is ever overlooked, and they tackle each mystery with _____ and _____. Over the years countless mysteries and mystery characters have been introduced to the reading and viewing public.

Review 1

These sentences include words from the previous four units.

Sentence Completion

Circle the word pair that best completes the meaning of the sentence.

1. The busy mother of three-year-old triplets was enjoying a
   _____ moment of quiet in contrast to the usual,
   _____ noise of living with three toddlers.

   A. obvious/fleeting
   B. rarefied/unremitting
   C. periodic/perpetual
   D. genuine/incidental
   E. conspicuous/sporadic

2. The injured passenger was barely _____; he stared at
   the young female police officer with_____ clearly
   showing on his face.

   A. apparent/irrelevance
   B. resistant/insistence
   C. coherent/perplexity
   D. lucid/perceptibility
   E. noteworthy/veracity

3. When you write a composition, you want to edit out all _____ words because most people prefer to read something that has _____ and conciseness.

   A. inconsequential/clarity
   B. discernible/legitimacy
   C. applicable/extraneous
   D. immaterial/semblance
   E. contingent/illusion

4. The warm front was only _____; we were living near the Canadian border, and it was (a) _____ to think that winter would be over in late February.

   A. short-lived/momentous
   B. imaginative/legitimate
   C. fleeting/abstruse
   D. indefatigable/pother
   E. transitory/fantasy

5. It is important that senior citizens have _____ checkups with their doctors in order to rule out the possibilities of their having developed _____ diseases such as diabetes.

   A. contingent/momentous
   B. valid/inconsequential
   C. periodic/chronic
   D. authentic/erroneous
   E. portentous/short-lived

ANSWERS

1-B, 2-C, 3-A, 4-E, 5-C.

SECTION III

Beauty and the Beast

We have myriad words to describe the beautiful and lovely. It takes only a few moments of thumbing through a contemporary woman's magazine such as *Glamour* or *Vogue* to read about all the ways the readers can become more *gorgeous,* more *radiant,* and ever more *irresistible.*

Unfortunately, every rose has a thorn, and this thorn might be a *churlish, crass,* or *depraved* creature that is trying to destroy all that is lovely and beautiful. Whatever the case, below you will find a surplus of words to describe them both.

alluring	gorgeous	resplendent
appealing	luminous	salacious
beaming	lustrous	scintillate
comely	pulchritude	striking
dazzling	radiant	
exquisite	ravishing	

· ·

barbarian	crass	Neanderthal
bestial	depraved	oafish
boorish	feral	rude
brutish	gross	uncouth
churlish	ill-bred	vulgar
coarse	loutish	

► **alluring**
adjective

Highly, often subtly attractive.

In her early years, Katharine Hepburn was considered an *alluring* star.

Verb: **allure**
Adverb: **alluringly**

► **appealing**
adjective

Attractive and inviting.

The job was very *appealing;* the hours and the tasks seemed totally suited to me.

Verb: **appeal**
Adverb: **appealingly**

► **beaming**
adjective

The state of being radiant; showing pleasure and happiness; shining.

My grandmother's *beaming* smile assured me that I had chosen the right birthday present for her.

Noun: **beam**
Verb: **beam**

► **comely**
adjective

Wholesome in appearance; attractively pleasing in looks and/or behavior.

Moira was a *comely* young woman; the men in the village were in awe of her good looks.

Noun: **comeliness**

► **dazzling**
adjective

Blinding in extravagance or beauty; amazing and overwhelming.

Her rhinestone-studded, shimmery gown enhanced Natalie's *dazzling* entrance to the party.

Verb: **dazzle**
Noun: **dazzler**

► **exquisite**
adjective

Characterized by unusual and often intricate beauty or design; intense; keen.

Clara's new engagement ring was an *exquisite* two-carat diamond in an unusual setting.

Noun: **exquisiteness**
Adverb: **exquisitely**

► **gorgeous**
adjective

Dazzlingly beautiful or magnificent; (less formal) wonderful, even delightful.

Because of the atmospheric conditions, the evening's sunset was *gorgeous.*

Noun: **gorgeousness**
Adverb: **gorgeously**

► **luminous**
adjective

• Having to do with light or emitting light.

Henrietta's skin was *luminous* in the candlelight.

• Seeming to be glowing with beauty.

The model's *luminous* beauty was evident through all of her stage makeup.

Noun: **luminosity**
Adverb: **luminously**
Verb: **illuminate**

► **lustrous**
adjective

Brilliant; lovely; outstandingly glowing and unusual.

Her long, freshly washed hair was *lustrous.*

Adverb: **lustrously**
Noun: **lustrousness**

► **pulchritude**
noun

Extreme beauty and unusual appeal.

The *pulchritude* of the young starlet overwhelmed the audience when she stepped onto the stage.

Adjective: **pulchritudinous**

► **radiant**
adjective

• Emitting heat, light, or radiation.

The room was kept warm by *radiant* heat.

• Beaming; overwhelmed by pleasure or extreme beauty.

Her beauty was enhanced by her *radiant* smile.

Adverb: **radiantly**
Noun: **radiance**

► **ravishing**
adjective

Extremely attractive; entrancing.

Without a doubt the young woman was a *ravishing* beauty.

Adverb: **ravishingly**
Noun: **ravishment**

► **resplendent**
adjective

Splendid or dazzling in appearance; brilliant.

The groom was *resplendent* in his tuxedo and ruffled, formal shirt.

Adverb: **resplendently**

► **salacious**
adjective

Appealing, especially in a sexual or even lewd manner.

The stranger's *salacious* glance made it clear just what his intentions were.

Noun: **salaciousness**
Adverb: **salaciously**

► **scintillate**
verb

To sparkle or shine, even to send off sparks or flashes.

The boring professor gave a far from *scintillating* lecture.

Adjective: **scintillating**
Adverb: **scintillatingly**

► **striking**
adjective

Extremely noticeable; outstandingly attractive or significant.

Because the model was very dark and nearly 6 feet tall, she was a very *striking* woman.

Adverb: **strikingly**

► **barbarian**
noun

A fierce, insensitive, cruel, or uncultured person.

Bruce was so unsophisticated that his behavior was like a *barbarian.* During the formal dinner, he ate his entire meal with his spoon, and he chewed with his mouth open.

The *barbarians* waged war upon those who were trying to civilize them.

Noun: **barbarianism**
Adjective: **barbarian, barbaric**

Bruce is *barbaric* in his eating habits.

► **bestial**
adjective

Marked by brutality; lacking reason or humanity; depraved and beastly.

A recent science fiction movie featured an entire caste of *bestial* characters whose images are being reproduced on plastic tumblers at the local carryout franchise.

Noun: **bestiality**
Adverb: **bestially**

► **boorish**
adjective

Rude and clumsy; lacking polish, courtesy, or humanity.

Raymond's character had become so *boorish* that his friends stopped asking him to go anywhere with them because he embarrassed them.

Noun: **boor**
Adverb: **boorishly**

► **brutish**
adjective

Crude in feeling; coarse; rough; uncivilized.

The character Hannibal Lector had to be totally restrained because of his **brutish,** cannibalistic actions.

Noun: **brute**
Adverb: **brutishly**

► **churlish**
adjective

Boorish; vulgar; of a dark nature; uncouth and uncivilized.

When the young man's attitude became **churlish,** he was quickly reprimanded by his father.

Noun: **churl**
Adverb: **churlishly**

► **coarse**
adjective

Rough; uncouth; not very civilized or polished.

The uneducated mountain man had a **coarse** way about him, but under it all he was very gentle.

Noun: **coarseness**
Adverb: **coarsely**

► **crass**
adjective

Crude; unrefined; lacking sensibility.

Despite his rather **crass** mannerisms, he had a tender heart and an understanding way about him.

Noun: **crassness**
Adverb: **crassly**

► **depraved**
adjective

Morally corrupt; morally unconventional, even perverted.

Many of the inmates in that part of the prison are *depraved* people, which is often a result of their dysfunctional upbringings.

Verb: **deprave**
Adverb: **depravedly**
Noun: **depravity**

► **feral**
adjective

Untamed, uncouth, and uncivilized; suggestive of an animal state of existence.

Although we thought we had domesticated the half-wolf, half-dog, when he smelled blood, he turned *feral* and started growling and gnashing his teeth.

► **gross**
adjective

Offensive; disgusting; without sensitivity or sophistication.

The crime scene was incredibly *gross;* everyone was relieved when the lieutenant said the investigation would be suspended until daylight.

Noun: **grossness**
Adverb: **grossly**

► **ill-bred**
adjective

Poorly brought up; impolite; unpolished; crude.

Because she had no parents and had grown up largely on her own, Tana was *ill-bred,* but she learned quickly in her new home because she didn't want to upset anyone.

► **loutish**
adjective

Having characteristics of an awkward or stupid person.

Although her actions were occasionally *loutish,* Kristie became more and more adept in social situations.

Noun: **loutishness, lout**
Adverb: **loutishly**

► **Neanderthal**
noun, adjective

Noun: An extinct human species; early homo sapien.

Anthropologists have found much evidence of *Neanderthal* man in the region of Dusseldorf, Germany.

Adjective: Crude, boorish, or awkward.

Some bachelors live such crude and basic lives that women view them as *Neanderthals.*

► **oafish**
adjective

Clumsy, stupid, crude, or awkward in behavior or demeanor.

At 6 feet 6 inches, Larry was often *oafish* in a small space, but on a basketball court he was poetry in motion.

Noun: **oaf**
Adverb: **oafishly**

► **rude**
adjective

- Relatively undeveloped or primitive.

The furniture was *rude* in its design, reflecting that specialized tools were not used when it was built.

- Ill-mannered and discourteous.

The child's *rude* behavior suggested that his parents were inadequate role models for behavior and decorum.

Noun: **rudeness**
Adverb: **rudely**

► **uncouth**
adjective

Crude and unrefined; awkward, clumsy, and/or ungraceful.

The basketball player's *uncouth* behavior got him thrown out of the game.

Noun: **uncouthness**
Adverb: **uncouthly**

► **vulgar**
adjective

Common and ordinary; unrefined and unpolished.

The child's *vulgar* language surprised his grandmother; she couldn't believe he would use such language in front of her.

Noun: **vulgarity**
Adverb: **vulgarly**

Sentence Completion

Circle the word or word pair that best completes the meaning of the sentence.

1. The auburn-haired model had _____ skin that seemed to glow from within.

    A. luminous
    B. comely
    C. beaming
    D. dazzling
    E. appealing

2. The diamonds on display at the jewelry store were _____ in their gleam and glimmer; I was overwhelmed by their purity.

    A. lustrous
    B. appealing
    C. striking
    D. salacious
    E. radiant

3. Monica's most _____ feature is her _____ smile.

    A. striking/beaming
    B. churlish/comely
    C. gorgeous/brutish
    D. feral/oafish
    E. scintillating/rude

4. Today, most expensive shampoos guarantee _____ hair and a _____ shine.

   A. luminous/coarse
   B. radiant/lustrous
   C. comely/scintillating
   D. vulgar/uncouth
   E. ravishing/ill-bred

5. The morally _____ creature was so crude and untamed that his actions indicated _____ behavior.

   A. appealing/oafish
   B. striking/barbarian
   C. crass/coarse
   D. churlish/boorish
   E. depraved/feral

Quick Matching

Write the letter of the definition shown in the right column next to the word that matches it in the left column.

_____1. Neanderthal	A. entrancing and attractive
_____2. bestial	B. crude and unrefined
_____3. crass	C. sparkling with energy
_____4. scintillating	D. marked by brutality; lacking humanity
_____5. ravishing	E. possessing prehistoric behavior

Complete the Story

Using these words selected from this unit, fill in the blanks to complete the story.

vulgar	gorgeous
reprehensible	exquisite
appeal	boors
ill-bred	salacious
dazzling	rude
oafish	depraved
lustrous	comely
beaming	feral
coarse	pulchritude
resplendent	

Children's fairy and folk tales are often more extreme than contemporary Golden Book and Disney presentations might indicate. Grimm's *Fairy Tales*, for instance, were often dark and somewhat _____ tales with _____ characters who were frequently uncivilized _____ identified by their _____ behavior and/or actions. Some of the "bad characters" are even _____ beasts who prey on the innocent, such as the wolf in "Little Red Riding Hood." The little girl in "The Red Shoes," had to have her feet removed to free her of the curse of the shoes!

In contrast to such _____ characters and _____ behavior are the "good characters" whose _____ is sometimes so extreme that their _____ becomes _____. The story of Cinderella, for instance, found in many cultures, is a _____ lass who must slave under the jealous eye of her _____ stepsisters and

_____ stepmother. Nevertheless, when the magic moment arrives, this girl turns into an _____ princess, _____ in gown and tiara, with _____ hair, _____ skin, a _____ smile, and a jubilant, _____ prince ready to do her bidding.

ANSWERS

Sentence completion: 1-A, 2-E, 3-A, 4-B, 5-E.

Quick matching: 1-E, 2-D, 3-B, 4-C, 5-A.

Complete the story: depraved, reprehensible, boors, coarse, feral, vulgar, rude, pulchritude, appeal, salacious, comely, oafish, ill-bred, exquisite, resplendent, lustrous, gorgeous, dazzling, beaming.

Smart as a Tack or Dumber than Dirt

Have you ever noticed that major characters in television sitcoms tend to come in two types? They are either *imprudent buffoons* whose *ludicrous* antics and *injudicious* decisions are often the result of *rash* or *witless* thinking, or they are clever characters who demonstrate *politic discernment* with a *keen, perceptive* outlook on life. Their incredible *sagacity* is too perfect to be believed. They are the Dudley Do Rights of television.

Few sitcoms give viewers characters who are well balanced or "normal" or who have any depth to them. What we see instead are characters whose personalities are too extreme to be realistic. You can't do much about the quality of television characters, but at least now you will have a selection of many words to describe and categorize each of them.

acumen	judicious	prudent
acute	keenness	sagacity
astute	perceptive	sapience
canny	perspicacity	shrewd
discernment	politic	

• •

buffoon	inane	preposterous
fatuous	indiscreet	rash
folly	inexpedient	witless
imprudent	injudicious	
inadvisable	ludicrous	

▶ **acumen**
noun

Keenness of mind; good insight; quickness; accuracy.

Fatima's mathematical *acumen* was so sharp that she did not find her calculus class difficult at all.

▶ **acute**
adjective

Clever; sharp of mind; incisive.

Her mother's hearing was so *acute* that Martha was usually caught when she tried to sneak in after curfew.

Adverb: **acutely**
Noun: **acuteness**

▶ **astute**
adjective

Clever and insightful; having an innate ability to understand or perceive.

The grandmother had *astute* intuition so she knew exactly when her grandchildren had done something wrong.

Noun: **astuteness**
Adverb: **astutely**

▶ **canny**
adjective

Careful; shrewd; clever; wily; full of guile.

Because Robert was so *canny,* no one could get away with anything when he was around.

Noun: **canniness**
Adverb: **cannily**

► **discernment**
noun

Keenness of insight and judgment.

Sammy solved the problem using insight and *discernment.*

Verb: **discern**
Adjective: **discerning**

► **judicious**
adjective

Having sound and prudent judgment.

The older lawyer was *judicious* in his advice to the young legal intern.

Adjective (alternative:) **judicial**
Adverb: **judiciously**

► **keenness**
noun

Smartly cutting or marked by remarkable mental quickness or understanding.

Anthony displayed such mental *keenness* that his friends always turned to him in times of distress.

Adverb: **keenly**
Adjective: **keen**

► **perceptive**
adjective

Having a keen sense of understanding and discernment.

Mr. Johnson is a *perceptive* teacher; he usually recognizes when one of his students is struggling with personal problems.

Verb: **perceive**
Adverb: **perceptively**

▶ **perspicacity**
noun

Acuteness of perception, discernment, or understanding.

Sara's *perspicacity* enabled her to solve the problem before anyone else.

Adjective: **perspicacious**
Adverb: **perspicaciously**

▶ **politic**
adjective

Prudent, expedient, and shrewd and artful.

Being *politic* as usual, Graciella was careful not to lose her temper even though the situation had angered her greatly.

Adverb: **politicly**

▶ **prudent**
adjective

Wise and careful; economical and exercising good judgment.

Muhammad was *prudent* with his allowance; he spent just enough to cover his basic needs.

Noun: **prudence, prude**
Adverb: **prudently**

▶ **sagacity**
noun

The quality of being discerning, sound in judgment, and farsighted; wisdom.

Officer Eugene's *sagacity* was amazing; he was easily able to figure out what was going on before the rest of the security squad had even assembled.

Noun: **sagacious**
Adverb: **sagaciously**
Adjective: **sage**

► **sapience**
noun

Unusual intelligence and extraordinary discernment.

George's *sapience* made him a natural for the detailed intelligence work required by his government.

Adjective: **sapient**
Adverb: **sapiently**

► **shrewd**
adjective

Characterized by being cunning, sharply intelligent, and even tricky or calculating.

Our Siamese cat is a *shrewd* animal; she holds perfectly still until the squirrels forget she's there. Then she pounces.

Noun: **shrewdness**
Adverb: **shrewdly**

• •

► **buffoon**
noun

A person given to clownish or foolish behavior; someone who is ludicrous and behaves stupidly.

The security person was such a *buffoon* that the intruders easily convinced him of their legitimacy and managed to burglarize all the offices.

Noun: **buffoonery**

► **fatuous**
adjective

Smugly and seemingly unconsciously foolish; delusive; prone to impossible speculation.

Eloise was *fatuous* and believed that by dyeing her white hair red she could regain the beauty and sparkle of her youth.

Noun: **fatuousness**
Adverb: **fatuously**

► **folly**
noun

A lack of good sense or foresight; an instance of foolishness or rash behavior.

The *folly* of his youth caught up with him when he tried to get into college and his low high school grades and poor attendance record led to his rejection by all the schools he applied to.

► **imprudent**
adjective

Unwise and indiscreet.

Mariah's *imprudent* behavior got her into trouble when her parents found out what she had been doing.

Noun: **imprudence**
Adverb: **imprudently**

► **inadvisable**
adjective

Unwise and ill-considered, especially considering immediate circumstances.

Despite the action of many ice fishermen, it is *inadvisable* in northern states such as Minnesota and upper Michigan to drive a car onto a frozen lake after the first of March.

Noun: **inadvisability**

► **inane**
adjective

Lacking sense, substance, or logic.

Karl's comments were so often *inane* that no one listened to him anymore.

Adverb: **inanely**

▶ **indiscreet**
adjective

Lacking discretion or good judgment.

The politician's *indiscreet* behavior made him the target of Jay Leno's monologues long after he left office.

Noun: **indiscretion**
Adverb: **indiscreetly**

▶ **inexpedient**
adjective

Inadvisable; unwise, hindering.

The commander's orders were so *inexpedient* that even the lowest-ranking soldiers knew they were following a fool.

Noun: **inexpediency**
Adverb: **inexpediently**

▶ **injudicious**
adjective

Showing a lack of discretion or good judgment; unwise.

Henri's *injudicious* behavior, such as driving the wrong way down a one-way street, often got both of us in trouble, even though I was usually just along for the ride.

Adverb: **injudiciously**

▶ **ludicrous**
adjective

Foolish for laughable or hilarious reasons.

Nathan's solution to the problem was so *ludicrous* and improbable that we thought it just might work.

Noun: **ludicrousness**
Adverb: **ludicrously**

► **preposterous**
adjective

Contrary to common sense; foolish; not natural.

Gloriana's suggestion was **preposterous;** we couldn't believe that anyone could come up with such a ridiculous idea.

Adverb: **preposterously**

► **rash**
adjective

Hasty, poorly planned, and not well thought out; foolish.

The coach's anger at his quarterback caused him to pull the player from the game, and many fans claimed that it was this **rash** decision that caused the loss of the championship game.

Noun: **rashness**
Adverb: **rashly**

► **witless**
adjective

Lacking intelligence, wit, or good sense.

The bystander was a **witless** witness for the prosecution; he could not even recall if the accident took place during the day or at night.

Noun: **witlessness**
Adverb: **witlessly**

Sentence Completion

Circle the word or word pair that best completes the meaning of the sentence.

1. The U.S. purchase of Alaska was nicknamed Seward's _____, after Seward, who was responsible for what many considered a worthless purchase.

   A. inanity
   B. witlessness
   C. folly
   D. keenness
   E. sagacity

2. The _____ fox seemed to know exactly how to evade the hunters.

   A. canny
   B. judicious
   C. perceptive
   D. prudent
   E. shrewd

3. The new ruling was so _____ that few people could vote for such a _____ thing.

   A. preposterous/ludicrous
   B. injudicious/shrewd
   C. sapient/inane
   D. astute/judicious
   E. acute/keen

4. The experienced lawyer's mental _____ made him a fair and _____ judge.

   A. acuteness/rash
   B. witlessness/acute
   C. prudence/indiscreet
   D. politic/preposterous
   E. acumen/judicious

5. The circus clown's _____ antics demonstrated what a _____ he was.

   A. inadvisable/sage
   B. witless/buffoon
   C. rash/wit
   D. astute/prude
   E. shrewd/inanity

Quick Matching

Write the letter of the definition shown in the right column next to the word that matches it in the left column.

_____1. prudent	A. lacking good judgment
_____2. rash	B. unusually perceptive
_____3. keen	C. showing good judgment
_____4. injudicious	D. quick and mentally incisive
_____5. perspicacious	E. hasty and poorly planned

Complete the Story

Using these words selected from this unit, fill in the blanks to complete the story.

acumen	rash
shrewd	canny
sagacity	discernment
inane	sapient
astute	ludicrous
fatuous	folly
rash	perspicacious
injudicious	buffoon
keen	

_____ television marketers have realized that the _____ slapstick routines of early comedy teams such as Laurel and Hardy and the Three Stooges would not be successful with today's viewing audiences. Their _____ and _____ of public viewing tastes resulted in the long-running animated show known as *The Simpsons*.

The Simpsons are a curious family of five characters, four of whom are the center of much public amusement and sometimes private criticism. Homer Simpson, the father, is a _____ who means well, but whose _____ decisions and _____ behavior bring much humor to the program. In contrast to him is his wife Marge. Sometimes she is a _____ woman whose _____ mind acts as a good foil to husband Homer. However, she often finds herself in _____ situations with hilarious outcomes.

The baby of the family, who has not aged in the last dozen years, has no developed personality. However, the two older children, Bart and Lisa, make up for this. Bart is a mischievous boy whose _____ behavior and constant _____ keep the viewing audience entertained. Lisa is the smart, _____ member of this cartoon family. She demonstrates _____ and _____ understanding of almost every situation. She is a _____ observer of human nature, and, despite her youth, this wisdom offers a sharp, entertaining contrast to Bart's _____ actions.

ANSWERS

Sentence completion: 1-C, 2-B, 3-A, 4-E, 5-B.

Quick matching: 1-C, 2-E, 3-D, 4-A, 5-B.

Complete the story: perspicacious, inane, acumen, discernment, buffoon, injudicious, fatuous, shrewd, canny, ludicrous, rash, folly, astute, sagacity, sapient, keen, rash.

Roar Like a Lion or Mew Like a Kitten

Some people are quiet and unassuming, like a spring rain. In fact, you often wonder if anything is going on inside them at all. These are the calm, serene sorts who go through life making few waves. In contrast are those people who always let you know they are around; they remind you of a tornado. Sometimes, they're loud. Often they are demanding and even irritating in manner. Nevertheless, it takes both kinds of people—any many in between—to make our lives interesting.

assuage	levelheaded	serene
appease	mitigate	slack
composed	placate	sluggish
détente	placid	tranquility
dormant	quiescent	
imperturbable	repose	

• •

blatant	din	ostentatious
boisterous	discordant	strident
brattle	fractious	truculent
brawl	hubbub	turbulent
clamorous	obstreperous	vociferous

► **assuage**
verb

To lessen; to take the edge off; to tone down.

To *assuage* his hunger during the 50-mile bike trip, Marvin ate a granola bar.

Noun: **assuagement**

► **appease**
verb

To pacify or make tranquil; to calm down or settle something or someone.

The New Testament tells us that to *appease* the angry crowd that was demanding death, Pontius Pilot gave them Jesus of Nazareth as a sacrifice, and he released Barabbas.

Noun: **appeasement**

► **composed**
adjective

Serene and self-possessed; calm and not easily agitated.

Maria was so *composed* that working in a day care center after school rarely fazed her.

Noun: **composure**
Verb: **compose**

► **détente**
noun

A relaxing or easing of tensions between rivals, often, but not always, in a political sense.

After the war in Iraq, it will take persistent and clever efforts to establish a *détente* between the United States and France.

▶ **dormant**
adjective

Lying asleep or in a calm state, but having the suggestion of life or activity that is temporarily quiet.

The grizzly bear was hungry after its *dormant,* three-month sleep.

Sometimes cancer cells lie *dormant* for years before they become active.

Noun: **dormancy**
Adverb: **dormantly**

▶ **imperturbable**
adjective

Not easily shaken; calm, cool, and easygoing; slow to become excited.

Marsha was *imperturbable;* no matter what last-minute project her boss burdened her with, she remained unruffled.

Adverb: **imperturbably**
Noun: **imperturbability**

▶ **levelheaded**
adjective

Usually composed and in control; not easily rattled or swayed by differing opinions.

Because Jason is so *levelheaded,* my mother thinks he will be a good influence on me.

Noun: **levelheadedness**

► **mitigate**
verb

To moderate in force or intensity; to calm or cool down; to lessen in intensity.

Jerome was able to *mitigate* Tanya's anger by explaining the circumstances of his missing their date and promising to make it up to her the following weekend.

Noun: **mitigation**
Adjective: **mitigated**

► **placate**
verb

To appease, pacify, soothe, or make amends.

The young mother was temporarily able to *placate* the fussy child by distracting him with a lollipop.

Noun: **placation**
Adjective: **placatory**

► **placid**
adjective

Undisturbed, unflappable, calm, serene, and satisfied.

There is nothing more relaxing than to sit by a *placid* lake on a warm summer day with nothing to think about other than when to return home for dinner.

Adverb: **placidly**
Noun: **placidity, placidness**

► **quiescent**
adjective

Quiet; still; at rest; serene and calm.

The *quiescent* child was deceptive, for her high energy and incessant demands were only temporarily at rest.

Noun: **quiescence**
Adverb: **quiescently**

► **repose**
noun, verb

Noun: Quiet tranquility; the state of being at rest or asleep.

My grandfather's *repose* was evident because we heard gentle snoring coming from his recliner, where he had dozed off.

Verb: To lie down or to lie at rest.

The patient *reposed* on the couch with his injured leg elevated.

► **serene**
adjective

Quiet and unperturbed; unaffected by disturbance; at peace within oneself.

Alice was so *serene* that, at the championship football game, the noise and enthusiasm around her barely made an impression on her.

Adverb: **serenely**
Noun: **serenity**

► **slack**
adjective

Slow moving, even lacking in activity; sluggish and unproductive.

In the automobile industry, the weeks before the changeover to next year's models tend to be a *slack* time at the manufacturing plants, thereby allowing maintenance crews the opportunity to service the machinery.

Noun: **slack**
Adverb: **slackly**

When a dog is properly trained to walk on a leash, the leash should have plenty of *slack* in it.

► **sluggish**
adjective

Displaying little growth or movement; not making progress; seeming to be bottlenecked or clogged to prevent advancement.

Traffic on the highway was ***sluggish,*** so many drivers took nearby exits, trying to avoid the bottleneck.

Adverb: **sluggishly**
Noun: **slug**: a person who is lazy or very inactive.

On Saturdays my brother is a ***slug***; he rarely gets out of bed before noon.

► **tranquility**
noun

Harmony; silence; quiet serenity; undisturbed and peaceful.

Because Marta found such ***tranquility*** at the lake, she often went there to unwind when she was upset or stressed about her parents or schoolwork.

Adjective: **tranquil**
Adverb: **tranquilly**

· ·

► **blatant**
adjective

Unpleasantly loud; irritatingly showy or obvious.

The students displayed ***blatant*** disrespect for the principal when, after he had just spoken to them about proper behavior in the auditorium, they continued to whisper and carry on with no courtesy for the guest speaker.

Adverb: **blatantly**
Noun: **blantancy**

► **boisterous**
adjective

Rowdy, rambunctious, and possibly out of control.

The overtired kindergarteners, who had consumed too much sugar at the birthday party, were ***boisterous.***

Adverb: **boisterously**

▶ **brattle**
noun

A rattling and crashing sound.

The ***brattle*** of his armor made it impossible for the knight to sneak up on his enemy.

▶ **brawl**
verb, noun

Verb: To have a loud and boisterous disagreement, possibly even a fight, but more likely just upsetting the calm and quiet.

Stefan was suspended when he ***brawled*** on the playground three times in one week.

Noun: A loud, boisterous disagreement.

During the Superbowl, a ***brawl*** erupted at a local sports bar.

Adjective: brawling or brawly

By the end of three overtimes, the drunken, ***brawling*** crowd around the bar was disturbing everyone in the restaurant.

▶ **clamorous**
adjective

Characterized by a loud, even discordant, noise, outcry, or insistent, disturbing racket.

The sound of the ***clamorous*** fire alarm in the middle of the night was disruptive to everyone in the dorm.

Noun: **clamor**
Adverb: **clamorously**

► **din**
noun

Disorder and noise; tumult and confusion.

The *din* in the cafeteria during lunch period was so great that my friends and I couldn't have a conversation without our having to yell at one another.

► **discordant**
adjective

Clashing in ideas or sound or philosophies; harsh with conflict.

The *discordant* notes he played on the piano were unsettling to me, and the hair on the cat stood up and he began to hiss.

Noun: **discord**
Adverb: **discordantly**

► **fractious**
adjective

• Unruly and noisy.

The *fractious* pre-schoolers were out of control.

• Cranky or peevish.

The *fractious* child had missed her nap and was trying everyone's patience with her whining and snuffling.

Noun: **fractiousness**
Adverb: **fractiously**

► **hubbub**
noun

An upset or vehement protest or discontent; sometimes a loud, sustained noise.

The unexpected victory of the underdog soccer team created such a *hubbub* that the police were called in to quell the disturbances and prevent a riot.

► **obstreperous**
adjective

Noisy and boisterous; sometimes even aggressive or defiant.

The toddler's behavior became *obstreperous* when he refused to lie down for a nap.

Adverb: **obstreperously**
Noun: **obstreperousness**

► **ostentatious**
adjective

Showy; characterized by a need to be noticed, not always favorably.

The house was an *ostentatious* disaster of architecture—every possible ornament had been added to the design without regard to appropriateness or style.

Adverb: **ostentatiously**
Noun: **ostentation**

► **strident**
adjective

Loud and harsh; often grating and discordant; hard on the ears.

The *strident* tornado siren alerted everyone to the impending danger, and people went to their basements or safe rooms if they had them.

Adverb: **stridently**
Noun: **stridency**

▶ **truculent**
adjective

Tending to argue and disagree, often vehemently and with great noise and commotion.

The homeless man, who was usually quite easy-going, became *truculent* when someone tried to take over his comfortable spot under the bridge.

Noun: **truculence**
Adverb: **truculently**

▶ **turbulent**
adjective

• Violently upset or disturbed.

After the torrential rains, the water in the nearby creek was *turbulent* and swiftly swept away great tree limbs and other debris.

• Having a restless or even revolutionary character.

The political climate was so *turbulent* that the local tribal leader did not dare to leave the village for fear that someone else would be in control of it upon his return.

Noun: **turbulence**
Adverb: **turbulently**

▶ **vociferous**
adjective

Offensively loud and often given to demonstration of agitated emotions or agitated outcry.

The accused *vociferously* defended himself on the grounds of his being greatly provoked by the man whom he attacked.

Noun: **vociferousness**
Adverb: **vociferously**

Sentence Completion

Circle the word or word pairs that best completes the meaning of the sentence.

1. After lying _____ during the cold winter, the tulip and daffodil bulbs began to sprout beneath the warming soil.

   A. repose
   B. détente
   C. sluggishly
   D. dormant
   E. serenely

2. Normally quiet and _____, Jerome amazed everyone when he got into a noisy _____ at the Pizza Palace when some of his so-called friends started to taunt him after the football game.

   A. imperturbable/brawl
   B. fractious/din
   C. levelheaded/truculence
   D. quiescent/discord
   E. ostentation/hubbub

3. The high-strung young bronco became _____ during the rodeo; even the most experienced handlers were unable to bring him under control.

   A. turbulent
   B. truculent
   C. boisterous
   D. vociferous
   E. ostentatious

4. After the torrential spring rains, the slow and often
_____ creek became dangerously _____.

    A. slack/strident
    B. sluggish/turbulent
    C. serene/brawling
    D. composed/discordant
    E. placid/blatant

5. The ear-splitting _____ of the alarm created such a
_____ that no one could hear the fire marshal as he
gave orders to the firefighters.

    A. hubbub/brattle
    B. turbulence/discord
    C. clamor/din
    D. brawl/vociferousness
    E. stridency/détente

Quick Matching

Write the letter of the definition shown in the right column next to the word that matches it in the left column.

_____1. assuage	A. to moderate the force or intensity
_____2. mitigate	B. to lie down to rest
_____3. placate	C. to disagree in a loud and boisterous manner
_____4. repose	D. to lessen or tone down
_____5. brawl	E. to appease, pacify, soothe, or make amends

Complete the Story

Using these words selected from this unit, fill in the blanks to complete the story.

quiescent	truculent
boisterous	levelheaded
imperturbable	discord
placate	détente
din	placatory
serene	fractious
vociferously	placid
clamorous	composed

My Uncle Rondo recently served on a jury. The case was a complicated one, and there was so much conflicting evidence that the jury had a difficult time reaching a verdict. It was the makeup of the group, however, that made things especially difficult.

Uncle Rondo said that the first job the jurors had was to elect a foreperson for the group. This had to be a _____ person who would lead the group and not get carried away by emotional arguments. They decided on a retired air-traffic controller, who was calm and _____, not surprising when you consider that his career had demanded that he remain _____ under stressful conditions. Two young, quiet, office workers were also on the jury. One was laid back and _____, and the other had a _____ nature. Since Uncle Rondo is _____ himself and always likes everyone to get along, he liked these two right away.

In contrast to this calm, _____ group were four rather _____ jury members who often had to be reminded to get back to the business of the moment. In fact, Uncle Rondo said they got so loud and _____ one day that the bailiff had to come in to the room where they were working and quiet the _____. After that, these three settled down to the job at hand.

Unfortunately, however, there were also four _____ hotheads in the group. They were quick to disagree, and they would argue _____. A couple of times the foreperson had to _____ hurt feelings because of the _____ behavior of these people. Until these four settled down, it was hard for the jury to get anywhere. Eventually a _____ was reached; everybody resolved to avoid further _____, and the jury was able to complete its task.

Uncle Rondo said that he learned a lot about the law by being on a jury during the two weeks of the trial and the two weeks it took them to reach a verdict. However, what he found the most interesting was what happens when twelve strangers, with very different personalities, have to work together toward a common goal.

ANSWERS

Sentence completion: 1-D, 2-A, 3-B, 4-B, 5-C.

Quick matching: 1-D, 2-A, 3-E, 4-B, 5-C.

Complete the story: levelheaded, imperturbable, composed, serene, quiescent, placatory, placid, boisterous, clamorous, din, truculent, vociferously, placate, fractious, détente, discord.

Something Old, Something New

Young people generally do not like being referred to as young, and some older people don't like to be called old. Fortunately, our language offers myriad other words to satisfy our descriptive needs. Some are relatively acceptable; others are less so. Nevertheless, the following words will provide you with alternatives to describe the concepts of youth and old age.

budding	innovation	proselyte
burgeoning	naive	raw
embryonic	nascent	rudimentary
fledgling	neophyte	shaver
incipient	neoteric	stripling
initiate	postulant	untried

. . . .

antediluvian	gerontic	primitive
antiquated	hoary	primordial
archaic	obsolescence	seasoned
dateless	outmoded	superannuated
fossilized	passé	venerable
full-fledged	prehistoric	veteran
geriatric	primeval	

▶ **budding**
adjective

Having to do with new or developing circumstances or abilities.

The *budding* artist was excited about his first gallery show.

▶ **burgeoning**
adjective

Growing or developing; blossoming or flourishing.

The *burgeoning* business had a rocky beginning, but soon it became a solid company worth millions of dollars.

Verb: **burgeon**

▶ **embryonic**
adjective

Of or belonging to an embryo; early beginning; not yet formed or matured; rudimentary.

The bird was in its *embryonic* stage when the egg fell out of the nest onto the patio.

Noun: **embryo**

▶ **fledgling**
adjective

New or immature; not yet out of the nest; not experienced; rudimentary.

The *fledgling* foreign reporter was anxious to get his story so he did not take his own safety into consideration during the mission.

▶ **incipient**
adjective

Beginning to exist or appear; early in developmental stage.

The architect's plans were still in their *incipient* stage when the builder broke ground for the new structure.

Adverb: **incipiently**
Noun: **incipience**

► **initiate**
noun, verb

Noun: One who is being or has been initiated; one who has been introduced to or has attained knowledge in a particular field.

Verb: To begin or start a process; to get things going.

The *initiate* met the visitors at the door, ready to *initiate* them into the world of art.

Adverb: **initially**
Noun (variation): **initiation**

► **innovation**
noun

The act of introducing something or someone; something newly introduced.

Myra's *innovation* was so creative that everyone was enthusiastic about following it up.

Verb: **innovate**
Adjective: **innovative**

► **naive**
adjective

Untried and inexperienced; not knowledgeable or practiced.

The *naive* youngsters were easily led astray by the older students, while the teachers seemed oblivious to what was going on.

Noun: **naïveté, naiveness**
Adverb: **naively**

► **nascent**
adjective

Coming into existence, emerging.

The committee had several *nascent* ideas for the new project, but nothing was decided by the end of the meeting.

Noun: **nascence**
Adverb: **nascently**

▶ **neophyte**
noun

A recent convert; a novice or beginner.

The youngster was a mere **neophyte;** he had no experience but only a mind full of dreams.

▶ **neoteric**
adjective

Of recent emergence; beginning; modern.

The ideas were **neoteric,** and because they had never been tried or tested, many of them were useless.

▶ **postulant**
noun

New to a situation; a petitioner or someone who is starting out on a new endeavor.

The **postulant** nun had just joined the convent, and she found that following all the rules was more difficult than she had ever imagined.

▶ **proselyte**
noun

A newcomer or someone newly converted; novice or beginner.

The Brownie scout was a true **proselyte** of the Girl Scouts—she couldn't wait to put on her uniform and start selling cookies.

Verb: **proselytize**

▶ **raw**
adjective

Uncooked or untried; inexperienced; unpracticed; experimental.

The new Marine recruits were so **raw** that their buzz haircuts sat uncomfortably on their heads.

Noun: **rawness**
Adverb: **rawly**

▶ **rudimentary**
adjective

Elementary; being in the earliest stages of development.

The students' knowledge of math was *rudimentary* since they could barely do more than add and subtract.

Noun: **rudiment**

▶ **shaver**
noun

Informal, somewhat colloquial expression used to describe a young boy; one without experience.

Many critics view Huckleberry Finn as a young *shaver,* out of his league in his journey down the Mississippi River; other critics recognize Huck as the mouthpiece of Mark Twain himself.

▶ **stripling**
noun

An adolescent male.

Every action of the seasoned hunters was closely observed by Georgio's nephew, a *stripling* who accompanied the men on their hunting trip.

▶ **untried**
adjective

Not tried or experienced; fledgling; without skill or knowledge.

The young retriever was *untried,* but she did a good job of retrieving on her first duck hunt.

▶ **antediluvian**
adjective

Extremely old; usually, historically a reference to the era before the Flood.

The forest was *antediluvian;* some of the trees had been alive since the prehistoric times.

► **antiquated**
adjective

Too old to be fashionable or contemporary in thinking or style; very old or aged.

The *antiquated* clothing at the Not New Shop attracted many partygoers on Halloween.

Verb: **antiquate**
Noun: **antiquatedness**

► **archaic**
adjective

Out of date; old; out of style, fashion, or contemporary thinking.

The equipment in the medical clinic was *archaic;* all of it had been purchased before 1970.

Adverb: **archaically**
Noun: **archaism**

► **dateless**
adjective

Having no date; so ancient that no date can be determined; having no limits in time; timeless.

The woman's dress was expensive, classic, and *dateless;* she might have worn it 30 years ago, or she might have purchased it in the last few months.

► **fossilized**
adjective

Converted to a fossil; made outmoded or inflexible with time.

The syrup had been in the pantry for so long that it had *fossilized* into a solid mass inside the bottle.

Verb: **fossilize**
Noun: **fossil**

► **full-fledged**
adjective

Fully developed or mature; attaining full rank, status, or experience.

The cadets had gone through months of boot camp until finally, upon graduation, they became *full-fledged* soldiers.

► **geriatric**
adjective

Of or related to the aged or the aging process.

The medical intern concentrated her studies in *geriatric* research.

Noun: **geriatrics**
Adverb: **geriatrically**

► **gerontic, gerontological**
adjective

Of or relating to very old age; having to do with the last stage of life.

All the men playing chess, though *gerontic,* were quick and clever strategists.

Susan's *gerontological* studies gave her insight into her relationship with her great aunt who was 89 years old.

Noun: **gerontocracy, gerontology**

► **hoary**
adjective

White or gray, as with age; old and venerable with wisdom and age.

The old beggar nodded his *hoary* head when I put money into his outstretched hand.

► **obsolescence**
noun

Something out of use or need; a dying breed or of unnecessary or unimportant need.

The car's *obsolescence* was obvious because it could not run on lead-free gasoline.

Adjective: **obsolescent, obsolete**

► **outmoded**
adjective

Out of fashion; of no more use, need, or practicality.

Last year's styles may be *outmoded,* but Tanisha could not afford to replace her wardrobe.

► **passé**
adjective

Out of mode or fashion.

Although it is *passé* for a man to tip his hat to a woman, many people still consider it a gentlemanly gesture.

► **prehistoric**
adjective

Of or relating to prehistory; slang—old and out of touch.

Archeology is the study of *prehistoric* civilizations.

Adverb: **prehistorically**
Noun: **prehistory**

► **primeval**
adjective

From the earliest times or ages; original or ancient.

The *primeval* swamps of the Florida Everglades are the setting for many horror and monster movies.

► **primitive**
adjective

Primary or basic; of or relating to an earliest or original stage or state; primeval.

My aunt still owns a *primitive* black-and-white television set.

Noun: **primitiveness**
Adverb: **primitively**

▶ primordial
adjective

Early in the developmental stage; basic and ancient.

Many American horror movies rely on touching the *primordial* fear within the audience—that same feeling we have when things go bump in the night.

Adverb: **primordially**

▶ seasoned
adjective

Characterized by experience, skill, or practice.

The football player had been in the game for 15 years and was a *seasoned* veteran of the gridiron.

▶ superannuated
adjective

Retired or outmoded; no longer in use or needed.

The librarians took inventory of the shelves and discarded all the *superannuated* books and magazines.

▶ venerable
adjective

Worthy of respect or reverence; honorable

Many cultures consider their ancestors as *venerable* fonts of wisdom.

Noun: **venerability, venerableness**
Adverb: **venerably**

▶ veteran
noun

A person who is long experienced or practiced in an activity or capacity; often associated with past military personnel.

The aged *veterans* marched proudly in their old uniforms on the eleventh of November.

Sentence Completion

Circle the word or word pair that best completes the meaning of the sentence.

1. The _____ company got off to a rocky start, but soon business picked up and it was firmly grounded.

   A. incipient
   B. fledgling
   C. stripling
   D. dateless
   E. primitive

2. The _____ computer was not worth salvaging; it should have been replaced several years ago.

   A. primeval
   B. veteran
   C. obsolescent
   D. burgeoning
   E. incipient

3. My niece is a _____ ballerina; she has barely conquered the most _____ of moves.

   A. shaver/archaic
   B. budding/rudimentary
   C. primitive/superannuated
   D. neoteric/untried
   E. primeval/passé

4. The Egyptian mummy was _____; since it predated most of recorded history, it quickly became a(n) _____ example of antiquity.

A. prehistoric/full-fledged
B. hoary/primeval
C. embryonic/incipient
D. geriatric/hoary
E. outmoded/seasoned

5. The police officer was hardly a(n) _____; he had been with the force for over 25 years, and many referred to him as the _____.

A. fledgling/neophyte
B. initiate/proselyte
C. shaver/fossil
D. gerontic/geriatric
E. obsolescence/innovation

Quick Matching

Write the letter of the definition shown in the right column next to the word that matches it in the left column.

_____1. primeval   A. early developmental stage
_____2. dateless   B. late developmental stage
_____3. gerontic   C. ancient and original in origin
_____4. nascent   D. having no limits in time; timeless
_____5. incipient   E. emerging; coming into existence

Complete the Story

Using these words selected from this unit, fill in the blanks to complete the story.

full-fledged
rudimentary
primeval
neophyte
outmoded
fossilized
embryonic
stripling

superannuated
geriatric
dateless
antiquated
budding
postulant
primitive

Great Britain—England, Wales, Ireland, and Scotland—is a land of many contrasts. A visitor to this land can walk through _____ forests or a _____ metropolis on the same day. Great Britain's history is almost d_____. It boasts many fine examples of _____ civilizations. In fact, many _____ remains have been unearthed in peat bogs, and an archeological dig, known as Sutton Hoo, revealed the remnants of a _____ Anglo-Saxon ship and all its contents buried beneath the fields of a modest farmer. Treasures from this archeological dig included _____ weapons and _____ jewelry.

Cities such as London, Dublin, and Glasgow also provide many contrasts. _____, _____ travelers are usually amazed at these cities. They will find many conveniences along with _____ plumbing and air conditioning. Although Americans often find British amenities _____, there is no doubt that the nation is far from

_____. In fact, Great Britain seems _____ in contrast to the _____ "colonies."

Review 2

These sentences includes words from the previous four units.

Sentence completion

Circle the word pair that best completes the meaning of the sentence.

1. The _____ giant swamp lizard exuded a _____ odor as it came close to the hunters.

   A. alluring/perceptive
   B. obstreperous/nascent
   C. uncouth/sluggish
   D. primordial/feral
   E. shrewd/radiant

2. Although it was _____ to think that she could keep up with the other experienced riders, Marta was _____ in her determination not to fall behind, so she kept on pedaling, despite aching muscles.

   A. ludicrous/obstreperous
   B. prudent/discordant
   C. innovative/churlish
   D. inadvisable/levelheaded
   E. shrewd/novel

3. The young T-ball players were _____ when it came to the strategies of baseball, so they seldom demonstrated much _____ as to where to throw the ball.

   A. barbarians/folly
   B. resplendent/astuteness
   C. neophytes/acumen
   D. boisterous/indiscretion
   E. quiescent/sagacity

4. The factory was old, and much of the equipment was
_____; nevertheless, the new owner was _____
enough to see the potential of the location of the building
and the good reputation of the company name.

A. ostentatious/vulgar
B. outmoded/vociferous
C. untried/politic
D. archaic/perceptive
E. burgeoning/serene

5. Although the young woman was usually dressed in a rather
_____ manner, she demonstrated such _____ in
her job as a lawyer's assistant that he started turning to
her for advice.

A. coarse/indiscretion
B. salacious/perspicacity
C. placid/serenity
D. rash/boisterousness
E. obsolete/tranquility

ANSWERS

1-D, 2-A, 3-C, 4-D, 5-B.

SECTION IV

Unit 1   Friend or Foe ►accommodating, affable, amiable, amicable, compatible, complaisant, concurrent, congruent, convivial, cordial, genial, harmonious, like-minded, obliging ►aloof, arrogant, contemptuous, derisive, disdainful, egocentric, haughty, incongruous, pompous, priggish, reticent, sanctimonious, self-aggrandizing, self-righteous, self-satisfied, smug, supercilious **133**

Unit 2   Give or Receive ►abstemious, chintzy, closefisted, frugal, meager, mercenary, miserly, niggardly, parsimonious, penurious, provident, stingy ►altruistic, benevolent, bounteous, eleemosynary, lavish, magnanimous, munificent, openhandedly, philanthropy, selfless, self-sacrificing, unstinting **147**

Unit 3   Commend or Condemn ►acclaim, admirable, applaud, approbation, celebrate, citation, creditable, encomium, esteem, eulogy, extol, kudo, laudable, meritorious, panegyric, praiseworthy ►abominate, admonitory, berate, blameworthy, castigate, censurable, culpable, decry, denounce, deplore, deprecate, despise, disparage, excoriate, objurgate, reprehensible, reproachful, reprove **161**

Unit 4   Fortitude and Foolhardiness ►audacious, bravado, dauntless, defiance, fortitude, gallant, intrepid, plucky, resolute, stalwart, steadfast, tenacious, valiant, virago ►brash, capricious, daring, derring-do, foolhardy, hotheaded, impetuous, impulsive, insolent, madcap, offhanded, perilous, rash, reckless, temerity **175**

Unit 5   One Size Does Not Fit All ►dearth, diminutive, infinitesimal, insignificant, Lilliputian, meager, minuscule, minute, mite, negligible, paucity, petty, pittance, scant, scintilla, trifling, trivial ►ample, behemoth, Brobdingnagian, colossal, copious, gargantuan, humongous, immeasurable, incalculable, infinite, mammoth, monumental, plethora, prodigious, statuesque, surfeit, titanic **191**

Friend or Foe

How do we choose our friends? Generally we try to avoid people who are *arrogant* and full of themselves. *Smug* and *disdainful* folks do not usually choose to bother with us anyway. The last thing we want is to spend a lot of time with anyone who is *sanctimonious, self-righteous,* or *supercilious.* No one appreciates a holier-than-thou attitude from others.

What we prefer are *amiable* and *compatible* people to be our friends. Acquaintances are generally *convivial, genial* people whose personalities are *harmonious* with our own. Fortunately, our language gives us an abundance of words to describe both those people with whom we prefer to spend our time and those whom we prefer to avoid.

accommodating	complaisent	genial
affable	concurrent	harmonious
amiable	congruent	like-minded
amicable	convivial	obliging
compatible	cordial	

. . . .

aloof	haughty	self-aggrandizing
arrogant	incongruous	self-righteous
contemptuous	pompous	self-satisfied
derisive	priggish	smug
disdainful	reticent	supercilious
egocentric	sanctimonious	

► **accommodating**
adjective

Helpful and obliging.

The police officer was ***accommodating*** as he helped us figure out where we were going.

Adverb: **accommodatingly**
Noun: **accommodation**
Verb: **accommodate**

► **affable**
adjective

Easy and pleasant to speak to; approachable and gracious.

Possibly thinking ahead to her tip, the waitress gave us an ***affable*** smile as she took our order.

Adverb: **affably**
Noun: **affability**

► **amiable**
adjective

Friendly and agreeable in disposition; good-natured, likable, and sociable.

Because Yer was an ***amiable*** woman, she rarely met a person who didn't become her friend.

Adverb: **amiably**
Noun: **amiability**

► **amicable**
adjective

Characterized by or showing friendliness.

Lauren was so ***amicable*** that everyone seemed to like her.

Noun: **amicability**
Adverb: **amicably**

► **compatible**
adjective

Existing or performing in harmonious, agreeable, or congenial combination with another or others.

Amy and Ray are a *compatible* couple; not only are they husband and wife, but they are best friends as well.

Adverb: **compatibly**
Noun: **compatibility**

► **complaisant**
adjective

Exhibiting a desire or willingness to please; cheerfully obliging.

Because golden retrievers have a very strong need to please their masters, they are considered *complaisant* house pets.

Adverb: **complaisantly**
Noun: **complaisance**

► **concurrent, concurring**
adjective

In accordance with other things or persons; harmonious; in agreement.

Because the time of the history class was *concurrent* with the time of the English class, I had to make a choice.

The mother was glad to see her usually squabbling boys were *concurring* with one another.

Noun: **concurrence**
Verb: **concur**

► **congruent**
adjective

Being in sync with others; easily collaborating with another.

Louis and I were *congruent* in our thinking, so we worked well together on the science project.

Adverb: **congruently**
Noun: **congruence**

► **convivial**
adjective

Pleasant; fun to be with; sociable and friendly.

As people started introducing themselves and sharing stories with one another, the party developed a *convivial* atmosphere.

Adverb: **convivially**
Noun: **conviviality**

► **cordial**
adjective

Warm, sincere, friendly, and gracious.

The receptionist in the lobby was *cordial* when we asked her for information.

Adverb: **cordially**
Noun: **cordiality**

► **genial**
adjective

Having a warm, friendly, and gracious nature.

Despite her initial barking, the dog had a most *genial* nature and simply wanted to be petted.

Adverb: **genially**
Noun: **geniality**

► **harmonious**
adjective

Exhibiting a pleasant and easy demeanor; friendly and pleasant.

Even though the household contained a cat, dog, bird, and fish, not to mention three teenagers, the home could usually boast a *harmonious* atmosphere.

Adverb: **harmoniously**
Noun: **harmony**

► **like-minded**
adjective

Of the same mind; in harmony with another.

The twins were so *like-minded* that they agreed on most issues.

Adverb: **like-mindedly**

► **obliging**
adjective

Ready to do favors for others; easy and willing to get along with others.

My coworker was *obliging* about trading work shifts with me.

Adverb: **obligingly**
Verb: **oblige**

· ·

► **aloof**
adjective

Distant physically or emotionally; reserved and remote; at a distance but within view; apart.

Melissa was shy and seemed *aloof,* but that behavior was a defense against having to expose her timidity to others.

Adverb: **aloofly**
Noun: **aloofness**

► **arrogant**
adjective

Having or displaying a sense of overbearing self-worth or self-importance.

The *arrogant* media mogul acted as if she thought she was above the law.

Adverb: **arrogantly**
Noun: **arrogance**

► **contemptuous**
adjective

Manifesting or displaying strong dislike, scorn, or contempt.

The rising executive was so determined to climb the corporate ladder that he was *contemptuous* of the feelings of those he pushed aside so that he could advance.

Adverb: **contemptuously**
Noun: **contemptuousness**

► **derisive**
adjective

Mocking or scoffing.

Tom's *derisive* comment regarding the English teacher made it clear that he didn't think very highly of her.

Noun: **derision**
Adverb: **derisively**

► **disdainful**
adjective

Demonstrating disdain, excessive pride, or scornful superiority.

Lauren became so full of herself after being elected homecoming queen that her friends could no longer tolerate her *disdainful* attitude.

Adverb: **disdainfully**
Noun: **disdainfulness**

▶ **egocentric**
adjective

- Behaving as if the entire world revolves around oneself; totally selfish.

Because infants are incapable of doing anything for themselves and everyone else must respond to their needs and demands, they might be considered *egocentric.*

- A theory of philosophy in which one's own mind is the center of everything.

Paula's belief in *egocentric* philosophies made her a very self-centered person.

Adverb: **egocentrically**
Noun: **egocentric** (the person), **egocentricity**, **egocentrism**

▶ **haughty**
adjective

Being overwhelmingly proud, vain, and self-centered.

Siamese cats tend to be aloof, and some people consider them too *haughty* to be good pets.

Adverb: **haughtily**
Noun: **haughtiness**

▶ **incongruous**
adjective

Inconsistent; inappropriate; not correct or customary according to the circumstances.

It was *incongruous* to see Chaltu at the student council meeting after she had been so openly critical of the council's decisions in the past.

Adverb: **incongruously**
Noun: **incongruity**

► **pompous**
adjective

Displaying an exaggerated degree of dignity and self-importance.

The *pompous* customer said to the waiter, "I don't drink anything but bottled water from France."

Adverb: **pompously**
Noun: **pompousness**

► **priggish**
adjective

Displaying an overly affected or smug narrow-mindedness.

Sally was so caught up in her own self-importance that people started referring to her as being *priggish*.

Adverb: **priggishly**
Noun: **prig**

► **reticent**
adjective

Exceptionally restrained or reserved in mannerism or speech.

Because Alfredo was afraid he would say something stupid, he was *reticent* about joining the class discussion.

Adverb: **reticently**
Noun: **reticence**

► **sanctimonious**
adjective

Displaying excessive piety or a holier-than-thou attitude.

Trying to impress his girlfriend's parents, Jack put on a *sanctimonious* performance, even going to church with the family although he was a professed atheist.

Adverb: **sanctimoniously**
Noun: **sanctimony**

► **self-aggrandizing**
adjective

Enhancing or exaggerating one's own importance, power, or reputation.

Caught up in his new position as supervisor, Steve exhibited *self-aggrandizing* behavior, which was not appreciated by the staff who had to listen to his boasting.

Noun: **self-aggrandizement**

► **self-righteous**
adjective

Overly sure of one's moral convictions or pious position.

The early American preacher Jonathan Edwards is known for his *self-righteous* sermon, "Sinners in the Hands of an Angry God."

Noun: **self-righteousness**

► **self-satisfied**
adjective

Possessing satisfaction with oneself or one's accomplishments.

After winning the election, Veronica felt *self-satisfied* with her efforts.

Noun: **self-satisfaction**

► **smug**
adjective

Being self-satisfied; complacent with oneself.

Martha was obviously *smug* when she was the only student able to answer the teacher's question correctly.

Adverb: **smugly**
Noun: **smugness**

► **supercilious**
adjective

Displaying an overabundance of pride or vanity; extremely smug or pleased with oneself.

Roger was spoiled by doting grandparents who gave him everything, and he took *supercilious* pleasure in owning toys that his friends' families could not afford.

Adverb: **superciliously**
Noun: **superciliousness**

Sentence Completion

Circle the word or word pair that best completes the meaning of the sentence.

1. Ralph was always ready to preach his beliefs to others, and his _____ got on everyone's nerves.

   A. complaisance
   B. sanctimony
   C. reticence
   D. pompousness
   E. aloofness

2. Because he had stuttered all his life, Paul was _____ about signing up for a speech class when he got to college.

   A. supercilious
   B. smug
   C. aloof
   D. reticent
   E. complaisant

3. Nancy _____ preached her personal beliefs, feeling certain that her convictions were correct.

   A. smugly
   B. superciliously
   C. arrogantly
   D. haughtily
   E. self-righteously

4. The _____ professor, considering himself above such menial tasks, would not answer his own phone, even when he was closer to it than the nearest servant.

A. pompous
B. reticent
C. self-righteous
D. smug
E. aloof

5. _____ and _____, the actress quickly dropped all her friends after she made her first successful movie.

A. egocentric/aloof
B. complaisant/haughty
C. arrogant/disdainful
D. reticent/priggish
E. supercilious/sanctimonious

Quick Matching

Write the letter of the definition shown in the right column next to the word that matches it in the left column.

_____ 1. affable	A.	well-matched
_____ 2. self-aggrandizing	B.	expressing strong dislike
_____ 3. contemptuous	C.	reserved in manner
_____ 4. reticent	D.	pleasing to be with
_____ 5. compatible	E.	enhancing or exaggerating one's own importance

Complete the Story

Using these words selected from this unit, fill in the blanks to complete the story.

unobliging	disdainful
self-satisfied	haughty
accommodating	contemptuous
smugly	reticent
arrogant	supercilious

In the late 1300s in England, Richard II was king. He was far from being an _____ monarch. In fact, he was _____ very _____ in response to his subjects' needs. Consequently, during his reign, the peasants were not _____ about letting the king know of their discontent. Led by Wat Tyler, they tried to revolt. The young king, not tolerant of such action, was _____ and unsympathetic to the peasants' cause. He believed he was king by divine right, and his _____ attitude caused many people to hate him. Nevertheless, he felt very _____ about his position, _____ reminding the peasants that they would never be able to become more than what they were—peasants. Although he was able to subdue the Peasants' Revolt, he was so _____ that this attitude alienated even those who supported his royal position. While he was out of the country, his kingship was overthrown, and, upon returning, he was put into prison. His _____ attitude did not go over well there, and he was assassinated while in captivity.

ANSWERS

Sentence completion: 1-B, 2-D, 3-A, 4-A, 5-E.

Quick matching: 1-D, 2-E, 3-B, 4-C, 5-A.

Complete the story: accommodating, haughty, unobliging, reticent, disdainful, supercilious, self-satisfied, smugly, arrogant, contemptuous.

Give or Receive

Some people seem naturally generous and forthcoming—what is theirs is yours just for the asking. In contrast, others are more tightfisted and less willing to share. Likewise, situations can seem generous, or tight—often depending upon the perception of the person who is experiencing it.

abstemious	meager	parsimonious
chintzy	mercenary	penurious
closefisted	miserly	provident
frugal	niggardly	stingy

· ·

altruistic	lavish	philanthropy
benevolent	magnanimous	selfless
bounteously	munificent	self-sacrificing
eleemosynary	openhandedly	unstinting

► **abstemious**
adjective

- Eating or drinking in moderation.

The Puritans in colonial America were known for their *abstemious* way of life; not only did they refrain from excessive eating and drinking, but their everyday living was restricted to bare necessities.

- Restricted to bare necessities; simplified.

Their everyday life was so *abstemious* that the theaters were closed and the only social entertainment took place at lunch.

Adverb: **abstemiously**
Noun: **abstemiousness**

► **chintzy**
adjective

- Gaudy or tacky.

The woman's red plastic purse looked *chintzy* in contrast to her designer cocktail dress.

- Miserly; tightfisted; stingy.

In Charles Dickens's *A Christmas Carol,* Ebenezer Scrooge was so uncaring and *chintzy* that he thought he was doing Bob Cratchit a favor by letting him spend Christmas day with his family.

Noun: **chintz**

► **closefisted**
adjective

Unwilling to part with money; sometimes known as hardfisted or tightfisted.

In fact, Scrooge was so *closefisted* that he suggested giving Cratchit only half his pay for the one day a year the man had away from his job.

► **frugal**
adjective

Costing or spending little; sparing in cost or expenditure.

After my uncle lost his job, there was money only for bare necessities, so his entire family had to become much more *frugal.*

Adverb: **frugally**
Noun: **frugality, frugalness**

► **meager**
adjective

Scanty; deficient in quantity or extent; less than necessary.

Because of the terrible weather during the prime growing season, the harvest was too *meager* to feed all the members of the tribe.

Adverb: **meagerly**
Noun: **meagerness**

► **mercenary**
adjective, noun

Adjective:

• Motivated only by monetary or personal gain.

Tobe had *mercenary* motives when she visited her rich aunt; she figured the elderly woman would leave her something in her will.

Noun:

• One who is motivated only by monetary or personal gain.

• A person who hires himself or herself out to fight for a foreign army.

Many French Huguenots fought in the American Revolution as *mercenaries;* some fought on the side of the Colonies, and some for the British.

► **miserly**
adjective

Stingy and sparing; not generous or willing to share or to be sympathetic to the plight of others.

Never one to share his good fortune with others, Roscoe was so *miserly* that he cut all his family members out of his will.

Noun: **miser, miserliness**

► **niggardly**
adjective

Stingy and miserly; not willing to part with anything, especially money. (This word comes from the Scandinavian *nig*, meaning a stingy person.)

Thelma was so *niggardly* about money that she thought a twenty-five cent tip was more than enough to leave to the hard-working server who had served her a $15 dinner.

► **parsimonious**
adjective

Excessively sparing or frugal, cautious about any sort of spending.

Serge's friends were embarrassed by his *parsimonious* behavior, so they often paid for everything rather than have him count pennies all the time.

Noun: **parsimoniousness**
Adverb: **parsimoniously**

▶ **penurious**
adjective

- Unwilling to spend or spare any money.
- Unyielding, unprofitable.
- Poverty-stricken.

The man was so **penurious** that he asked his children to help him pay for groceries.

Adverb: **penuriously**
Noun: **penuriousness, penury**

▶ **provident**
adjective

- Careful and circumspect in one's behavior, especially concerning the future.
- Careful when spending money.
- Careful to look out for one's own interests.

Even when he was **provident** with his money, he never had enough to get him through each week.

Noun: **providence**
Adverb: **providently**

▶ **stingy**
adjective

- A common term describing someone who is tightfisted or miserly.
- Unyielding such as in barrenness in land or productivity.

Reluctant to help him out, however, his **stingy** children humiliated the old man by making him beg for every penny they gave him.

Noun: **stinginess**
Adverb: **stingily**

▶ **altruistic**
adjective

Truly generous and not concerned with self but concerned rather with the welfare of others.

The retired man was fortunate to come across a very successful old friend whose *altruistic* nature made him only too willing to help his old comrade.

Adverb: **altruistically**
Noun: **altruism**

▶ **benevolent**
adjective

Having goodwill and generosity, especially toward those less fortunate.

This *benevolent* friend was so easy-mannered that he never made the retired man feel the least bit embarrassed by his situation.

Adverb: **benevolently**
Noun: **benevolence**

▶ **bounteously**
adverb

Generously and copiously (in ample quantities) given.

In fact, this rich friend shared his good fortune so *bounteously* that the retired man was able to pay back his children and not have to feel humiliated ever again.

Adjective: **bounteous**
Noun: **bounteousness**

► **eleemosynary**
adjective

Generously given; benevolent. (Comes from the Latin, related to the word *alms,* money given to the poor.)

The retired man felt that he could never properly repay the ***eleemosynary*** generosity of his friend, but his friend reminded him that their friendship was worth more than anything money could ever buy.

► **lavish**
adjective

• Extravagant and profuse.

Miriam is a ***lavish*** hostess; nothing is too good or too much for her houseguests.

• Willing to give generously, often excessively.

The young bride planned a ***lavish*** wedding reception at which the food averaged about $120 per guest.

Adverb: **lavishly**
Noun: **lavishness**

► **magnanimous**
adjective

• Courageous and noble in heart and mind.

Sir Lancelot, although he loved Guinevere, was a ***magnanimous*** knight who respected the fact that she was Arthur's wife.

• Generous; willing to share one's bounty with others.

The father of the bride was a likable person with a ***magnanimous*** spirit, so all the guests felt welcome and comfortable around him.

Adverb: **magnanimously**
Noun: **magnanimity**

► **munificent**
adjective

Showing great generosity, often in a regal or princely manner.

The bride was fortunate to have a rich and *munificent* father who gave her whatever she wanted.

Adverb: **munificently**
Noun: **munificence**

► **openhandedly**
adverb

Liberally, generously, and freely bestowing upon others.

In fact, the reception was so excessive that the bride *openhandedly* gave each of the guests an expensive memento.

Adjective: **openhanded**
Noun: **openhandedness**

► **philanthropy**
noun

Goodwill; effort to promote human welfare.

Because of this father's *philanthropy* toward the city's chamber orchestra, the musicians were more than happy to play at his daughter's wedding reception.

Adverb: **philanthropically**
Adjective: **philanthropic**

► **selfless**
adjective

Not motivated by any concern for self, only for others; unselfish.

In order to be a good police officer or firefighter, one must be truly *selfless,* often putting oneself in danger in order to care for or protect others.

Adverb: **selflessly**
noun: **selflessness**

► **self-sacrificing**
adjective

Totally unselfish; willing to go beyond the norm to give to others.

Much of this *self-sacrificing* character was evident in those who helped during and after the 9/11 attack.

Adverb: **self-sacrificingly**

► **unstinting**
adjective

• Marked by lavish overabundance.

Charles was an *unstinting* suitor: He sent Valerie flowers and gifts all the time.

• Bestowed upon liberally, with much devotion and even self-sacrifice.

Hour upon hour, firefighters from New York and many from outside the city were *unstinting* in their efforts to recover survivors from the World Trade Center wreckage.

Adverb: **unstintingly**

Sentence Completion

Circle the word or word pair that best completes the meaning of the sentence.

1. Jonah's father was so _____ that during college Jonah had to hold two jobs in order to make ends meet.

   A. stingy
   B. penurious
   C. lavish
   D. benevolent
   E. altruistic

2. Pamela disliked the poorly made dress; she thought it looked _____.

   A. closefisted
   B. lavish
   C. chintzy
   D. munificent
   E. abstemious

3. Sasha was so _____ in her behavior that she was always helping others _____.

   A. openhanded/penuriously
   B. lavish/providentially
   C. provident/abstemiously
   D. bounteous/niggardly
   E. self-sacrificing/selflessly

4. Isaac's _____ personal spending enabled him to practice _____ for many worthy causes.

A. stingy/selflessness
B. unstinting/bounteousness
C. meager/lavishness
D. altruistic/frugality
E. self-sacrificing/munificence

5. Rachel _____ delivered food to the needy during the holidays; she acted _____, never expecting anything in return for her generous spirit.

A. openhandedly/magnanimously
B. philanthropically/selflessly
C. meagerly/frugally
D. benevolently/abstemiously
E. lavishly/unstintingly

Quick Matching

Write the letter of the definition shown in the right column next to the word that matches it in the left column.

_____1. altruistic   A. miserly

_____2. lavish   B. careful

_____3. provident   C. unstinting

_____4. parsimonious   D. bounteous

_____5. niggardly   E. frugal

Complete the Story

Using these words selected from this unit, fill in the blanks to complete the story.

meager	selflessly
frugal	parsimonious
openhanded	philanthropy
self-sacrificing	lavish
stingy	benevolent
magnanimous	abstemious
chintzy	unstinting
miserly	closefisted

Visiting my father's parents and visiting my mother's parents is a study in opposites. Overall, my father's family is very _____; none of them is willing to spend an extra dime on anything. In fact, they are so _____ and _____ that they often buy things of _____ quality that look cheap and _____. My grandfather is so _____ about every purchase that family get-togethers are far from _____. Even Thanksgiving dinners are quite _____. He acknowledges this character trait, however, and even he laughs at his own _____ spending behavior.

In contrast, my mother's family are the most generous and _____ people you'll ever meet. Every family gathering is _____ in food and drink. My mother's father is very _____; he always slips each grandchild $5 or $10. His generosity is also public; his _____ is often demonstrated by his _____ donations to the arts and to education. He's a _____ person who _____ not only gives his money but volunteers his time and services as well.

ANSWERS

Sentence completion: 1-A, 2-C, 3-E, 4-E, 5-B.

Quick matching: 1-C, 2-D, 3-B, 4-E, 5-A.

Complete the story: frugal, stingy, miserly, meager, chintzy, parsimonious, lavish, abstemious, closefisted, benevolent, unstinting, openhanded, philanthropy, magnanimous, self-sacrificing, selflessly.

Commend or Condemn

Every day in the news we hear stories about terrible situations that news commentors cannot condemn enough. They *denounce reprehensible* behavior, and they make *disparaging* comments about despicable public figures who are *blameworthy* for their *censurable* deeds instead of acting like the role models they ought to be. It seems that there are not enough words in our language to report such *deplorable* news.

On the other hand, the news occasionally celebrates *creditable* accomplishments and *extols* those whose *laudable* behavior is *praiseworthy* rather than *blameworthy*. The following words offer a wide selection of descriptors to help us both condemn and commend.

acclaim	creditable	laudable
admirable	encomium	meritorious
applaud	esteem	panegyric
approbation	eulogy	praiseworthy
celebrate	extol	
citation	kudo	

abominate	culpable	disparage
admonitory	decry	excoriate
berate	denounce	objurgate
blameworthy	deplore	reprehensible
castigate	deprecate	reproachful
censurable	despise	reprove

► **acclaim**
verb, noun

Verb: To applaud or congratulate with much enthusiasm; to strongly approve.

The coach will always *acclaim* his team whenever they perform well.

Noun: Enthusiastic applause or recognition.

The Olympic gold medal skater was met with much *acclaim* when he returned to his small native country.

Noun: **acclamation**
Adjective: **acclaimed**

► **admirable**
adjective

Worthy of being admired or respected.

Patrick's behavior was *admirable;* when the little girl ran in front of the car, he ran into the street and picked her up, saving her from probable disaster.

Verb: **admire**
Adverb: **admirably**
Noun: **admirability**

► **applaud**
verb

To express approval, often by the clapping of hands.

The high school principal *applauded* the teacher's quick response when a student had a seizure in her classroom.

Adjective: **applaudable**
Noun: **applauder, applause**
Adverb: **applaudably**

► **approbation**
noun

Expression of approval, often official in nature.

The mayor's *approbation* for solving the difficult case was helpful to the police department, which had been receiving negative publicity.

Verb: **approbate**
Adjective: **approbative, approbatory**

► **celebrate**
verb

• To praise or make widely known or creditable.

The family *celebrated* Shawna's success when she won a National Merit Scholarship.

• To observe certain seasons or festivities.

During fall and early winter many cultures *celebrate* a variety of religious holidays.

Noun: **celebration**
Adjective: **celebratory**

► **citation**
noun

Official commendation or recognition.

Moira received a *citation* for her exemplary behavior in a critical situation.

Adjective: **citational**

► **creditable**
adjective

• Deserving of often limited praise or accommodation.

His performance at the talent show was not the best he'd ever given, but it was *creditable.*

• Deserving of commercial credit or reputation.

Her supervisor told Sam that the new vendor was a *creditable* company, worthy of pursuing.

Noun: **credit**
Adverb: **creditably**

► **encomium**
noun

Warm, deserving praise; a tribute.

The squad commander gave the soldier an *encomium* for his brave and selfless action that saved three other lives.

► **esteem**
noun

Favorable respect or regard.

The learned professor was held in such *esteem* that his classes were always the first to fill at registration.

Adjective: **estimable**
Noun: **estimation**
Verb: **esteem**

► **eulogy**
noun

A laudatory speech written in praise of a person, usually after his or her death.

At the senator's funeral, several people gave *eulogies* mentioning his accomplishments.

Verb: **eulogize**
Adjective: **eulogistic**

► **extol**
verb

To praise highly.

The townspeople ***extolled*** the world-renowned hero when he returned to his home.

Nouns: **extoller, extolment**

► **kudo**
noun

Praise; a compliment.

Kudos go to the employee who came up with this innovative and practical suggestion.

► **laudable**
adjective

Worthy of praise and/or recognition.

Although his accomplishment was ***laudable,*** the man was humble in accepting the mayor's congratulations.

Noun: **laudableness, laudability**
Adverb: **laudably**

► **meritorious**
adjective

Deserving of award, merit, or praise.

During the aftermath of the 9/11 tragedy, many firefighters and police officers demonstrated ***meritorious*** behavior that made Americans proud.

Adverb: **meritoriously**
Noun: **merit**

► **panegyric**
noun

A formal public compliment or elaborate praise.

After all the statesman had done for his home state, there was much ***panegyric*** upon the news of his unexpected death.

Adjective: **panegyrical**
Adverb: **panegyrically**

► **praiseworthy**
adjective

Meriting praise and high commendation.

For 10 years in a row Isabel demonstrated *praiseworthy* behavior when she missed out on having dinner with her family in order to serve Thanksgiving dinner to the needy at the soup kitchen.

Adverb: **praiseworthily**
Noun: **praiseworthiness**

• •

► **abominate**
verb

To detest thoroughly.

Cinderella's stepsisters *abominated* her to the extent that they did everything they could to prevent her from attending the prince's ball.

Adjective: **abominable**
Noun: **abomination**
Adverb: **abominably**

► **admonitory**
adjective

Mildly cautionary, reproving, or scolding

My mother's *admonitory* tone let me know that she was unhappy with me, even though her words were not harsh.

Noun: **admonition**
Verb: **admonish**

► **berate**
verb

To scold angrily and at length.

Sean's mother was constantly *berating* him for keeping his room so messy.

► **blameworthy**
adjective

Worthy of blame or reproof; guilty; deserving punishment.

Since my friends and I had been playing ball in the yard, we were *blameworthy* when the ball shattered our neighbor's large front window.

Noun: **blameworthiness**

► **castigate**
verb

To criticize thoroughly, even to punish for an infraction.

After I broke the window, my father *castigated* me soundly and grounded me for a month.

Noun: **castigation**

► **censurable**
adjective

Deserving of censure or blame.

The *censurable* behavior of the sociopath Ted Bundy horrified the public.

Verb: **censure**

► **culpable**
adjective

At fault; deserving blame.

The crumbs stuck on his face made it easy to see that my little brother was *culpable* of raiding the cookie jar.

Noun: **culpability, culpableness**
Adverb: **culpably**

► **decry**
verb

To openly condemn.

The crowd loudly *decried* the traitor before he was executed.

Noun: **decrier**

► **denounce**
verb

To condemn, criticize, or accuse.

The court of King Henry VIII was quick to *denounce* Anne Boleyn as a traitor when Henry no longer wanted her as his wife.

Noun: **denouncement, denouncer, denunciation**

► **deplore**
verb

To express strong dislike or disapproval; to condemn.

Joe *deplored* his brother's illegal actions; he always knew that his brother's friends would eventually lead him to trouble.

Adjective: **deplorable**
Adverb: **deplorably**

► **deprecate**
verb

To belittle; express disapproval; deplore.

The hockey player's *deprecating* tone toward the referee was not tolerated, and he soon found himself sitting in the penalty box.

Noun: **deprecation**
Adjective: **deprecating**
Adverb: **deprecatingly**

► **despise**
verb

To look down on with contempt or scorn.

It was easy for Mary to *despise* her former friend after their argument.

Adjective: **despicable**
Adverb: **despicably**
Noun: **despiser**

► **disparage**
verb

To speak in a disrespectful way; to belittle; to reduce in esteem.

It is not unusual for opposing forces to *disparage* one another during a closely contested election.

Noun: **disparagement, disparager**
Adverb: **disparagingly**

► **excoriate**
verb

To censure severely; to denounce; to scold; to rebuke sharply.

After the public scandal, the press was quick to *excoriate* the congressman for his unethical behavior.

Noun: **excoriation**

► **objurgate**
verb

To scold sharply; to berate.

The judge was quick to *objurgate* the jury members when he found out that they had been watching television.

Noun: **objurgation**
Adverb: **objurgatorily**
Adjective: **objurgatory**

► **reprehensible**
adjective

Deserving rebuke, scolding, or censure.

The criminal's *reprehensible* behavior made it difficult for the defense lawyer to make much of an impression on the jury.

Noun: **reprehensibility**
Adverb: **reprehensibly**

► **reproachful**
adjective

Deserving reproach or blame.

After Ed got in trouble, he felt that his parents were always giving him *reproachful* looks.

Noun: **reproachfulness**
Adverb: **reproachfully**

► **reprove**
verb

To voice reproof or disapproval; to find fault with.

Shana frequently *reproved* the homecoming committee for not getting its float built as quickly as it should have.

Noun: **reproval, reprover**
Adjective: **reprovable**
Adverb: **reprovingly**

Sentence Completion

Circle the word or word pair that best completes the meaning of the sentence.

1. After returning from their successful mission, the four astronauts were given a presidential _____, which was televised nationwide.

   A. applause
   B. panegyric
   C. celebration
   D. denouncement
   E. disparagement

2. Henri was surprised by the principal's _____ tone because he knew that he was not responsible for what had happened and therefore not _____.

   A. admirable/creditable
   B. laudatory/laudable
   C. admonitory/blameworthy
   D. censurable/deplorable
   E. disparaging/esteemed

3. The Nobel Prize winner received national _____ and _____ for his incredible invention.

   A. acclaim/approbation
   B. applause/admonition
   C. abomination/approbation
   D. admiration/censure
   E. kudos/castigation

4. The biased talk show host _____ the congressman for his _____ behavior.

    A. extolled/deplorable
    B. decried/laudable
    C. acclaimed/reproachful
    D. castigated/reprehensible
    E. reproved/meritorious

5. During the funeral ceremony, the Army commander _____ the dead soldier's _____ action in battle.

    A. extolled/abominable
    B. objurgated/praiseworthy
    C. approbated/censurable
    D. berated/deplorable
    E. eulogized/meritorious

Quick Matching

Write the letter of the definition shown in the right column next to the word that matches it in the left column.

_____1. kudos	A. express approval
_____2. deplore	B. to openly condemn
_____3. decry	C. to scold
_____4. objurgate	D. praise and compliments
_____5. applaud	E. express disapproval

Complete the Story

Using these words selected from this unit, fill in the blanks to complete the story.

deplorable	excoriating
admirable	esteem
applaud	reprehensible
denounce	creditable
castigated	laudable
excoriate	celebrated
kudos	estimable

Recently, City Theatre presented an atypical but _____ interpretation of Shakespeare's *Richard III*. Shakespeare's King Richard III is not an _____ character. In fact, historians generally _____ his selfish, some think traitorous, behavior and _____ actions. He was the hunchbacked, physically impaired king who supposedly had his two nephews killed because he saw them as a threat to his position as king. For this he has been universally _____. In addition, he had his brother drowned, supposedly in a vat of wine— another _____ act.

The local stage production, however, portrays Richard in a better light, much less _____ than history would have him. This production has created a Richard that makes the audience almost feel sorry for him. The audience actually develops a tendency to _____ his courage, not berate him. Rather than a hunchback, this Richard is handicapped, and he stumps about the stage on crutches. The nimble actor uses the crutches to his advantage, often swinging from them, vaulting onto a low wall, and even using them as a makeshift weapon. The actor's outstanding performance makes the audience _____ Richard for how he copes with his deformity. Through implication and a bit of poetic license with a few of Shakespeare's original lines, we quickly gather that he is a victim to be _____ for his amazing coping abilities. He is set up—someone other than he is responsible for the deaths—and the audience quickly understands that, without his _____ wits and strong survival instinct, he too might become a victim.

Needless to say, critics are mixed in their reactions to this production. The purists are quick to _____ the director as unprofessional and as only interested in making money while cheapening the original intent of the play. The more open-minded viewers, however, find this interpretation refreshing. They claim this new interpretation is _____ and offer many _____ to all those responsible for this original production.

ANSWERS

Sentence completion: 1-B, 2-C, 3-A, 4-D, 5-E.

Quick matching: 1-D, 2-E, 3-B, 4-C, 5-A.

Complete the story: creditable, admirable, excoriate, reprehensible, castigated, deplorable, excoriating, esteem, applaud, celebrated, estimable, denounce, laudable, kudos.

Fortitude and Foolhardiness

O ften people are called upon to demonstrate courage because situations become *perilous*. Because there is a fine line between a hero and a fool, we have a variety of words to describe deeds of bravery and *daring*. Someone can easily possess *daring* but demonstrate it as *foolhardiness*. These distinctions are often based more on the perception of others than on the action itself.

audacious	gallant	steadfast
bravado	intrepid	tenacious
dauntless	plucky	valiant
defiance	resolute	virago
fortitude	stalwart	

. . . .

brash	hotheaded	offhanded
capricious	impetuous	perilous
daring	impulsive	rash
derring-do	insolent	reckless
foolhardy	madcap	temerity

▶ **audacious**
adjective

- Fearlessly bold; possibly even foolhardy and daring.

During the 9/11 tragedy, many *audacious* firemen gave their lives saving others.

- Unrestrained by convention or propriety; insolent.

Emily displayed her *audacious* spirit when she arrived at the prom wearing a tuxedo

- Spirited and original.

Hollywood producers did an *audacious* interpretation of Shakespeare's *Macbeth* when they made it into a gangster movie.

Noun: **audaciousness**
Adverb: **audaciously**

▶ **bravado**
noun

A tendency toward showy defiance or false expressions of courage.

Often soldiers must bolster their courage with showy displays of *bravado* in order to keep up their nerve.

▶ **dauntless**
adjective

Not easily intimidated; courageous and brave.

Many of the rescuers who worked at Ground Zero after 9/11 were *dauntless* in the face of danger and sorrow.

Adverb: **dauntlessly**
Noun: **dauntlessness**

▶ **defiance**
noun

• Bold resistance; brave opposition.

Defiance was evident in the eyes of the young boy as he withstood taunting and teasing from his classmates.

• Arrogant attitude, often rude and dismissive.

The disobedient child displayed his *defiance* when he stubbornly refused to obey his parents.

Adjective: **defiant**
Adverb: **defiantly**
Verb: **defy**

▶ **fortitude**
noun

Showing great strength and bravery under adverse conditions such as pain and torture.

Despite being grilled and tortured regularly by his captors, the POW colonel's *fortitude* and religious faith kept him alive.

► **gallant**
adjective

• Bold and dashing.

The *gallant* Sir Walter Raleigh is said to have laid his cloak across a puddle so that Queen Elizabeth would not get her shoes wet as she walked by.

• Bravely daring; selflessly courageous.

The soldiers at the battle of the Alamo made a *gallant* attempt to save the fort from their attackers, but not one of them managed to survive.

• Stately; majestic; seemingly regal in demeanor.

When the *Titanic* sailed from Queensland, Ireland, no one would have predicted that such a grand and *gallant* ship would suffer such a disastrous ending.

Noun: **gallantry**
Adverb: **gallantly**

► **intrepid**
adjective

Courageous; acting with much determination and little fear.

Neil Armstrong, the first man to walk on the moon, was an *intrepid* pioneer of the twentieth century.

Noun: **intrepidity, intrepidness**
Adverb: **intrepidly**

► **plucky**
adjective

Having or displaying courage, tenacity, and resourcefulness under difficult or trying circumstances.

After the accident that resulted in paralysis of most of his body, Christopher Reeve has demonstrated his *plucky* approach to life and his own handicap by turning his misfortune into a campaign to support research into paralysis.

Noun: **pluck, pluckiness**
Adverb: **pluckily**

► **resolute**
adjective

Firm, determined, and unwavering.

Martha was *resolute* in her determination to lose 10 pounds before the prom.

Adverb: **resolutely**
Noun: **resolution**
Verb: **resolve**

► **stalwart**
adjective

Strong, bold, daring, firm, and resolute; having determination and a stick-to-it attitude.

Though his actions were foolish, Don Quixote was a determined and *stalwart* pursuer of his dreams.

Adverb: **stalwartly**
Noun: **stalwartness**

▶ **steadfast**
adjective

Steady and reliable; dependable even during trying or dangerous times.

Because of unwavering devotion to its master or mistress, the golden retriever can be a *steadfast* companion.

Noun: **steadfastness**
Adverb: **steadfastly**

▶ **tenacious**
adjective

• Holding tight; not letting go or yielding to the opposition.

Margaret would not be dissuaded from her opinion; she was *tenacious* in her beliefs about *Roe v. Wade*.

• Having the characteristic of being cohesive and adhering well to other substances

Cat owners know how *tenacious* cat hair can be on their clothes and furniture.

Noun: **tenacity, tenaciousness**
Adverb: **tenaciously**

▶ **valiant**
adjective

Brave; full of valor and courage.

The *valiant* young bombardier was decorated with the Purple Heart for his heroic efforts during World War II.

Noun: **valiance, valiancy**
Adverb: **valiantly**

► **virago**
noun

- A woman who is noisy, bold, or domineering.

The fisherman's wife was a real *virago:* all she did was scold and nag her husband whenever he was home.

- A strong, often large, courageous, and brave woman.

Displaying undaunted courage in her fight for decent medical care for "her" soldiers, Florence Nightingale was a true *virago* during the Crimean War.

•••

► **brash**
adjective

Hasty, unthinking, and impetuous; quick to act without considering the consequences.

The teen made a *brash* decision to stay out all night with his friends, but he was ultimately sorry for causing his parents such concern.

Adverb: **brashly**
Noun: **brashness**

► **capricious**
adjective

Impulsive, whimsical.

In a *capricious* moment, the couple went to the next state and got married—an action they would regret for the rest of their lives.

Noun: **caprice**
Adverb: **capriciously**

▶ **daring**
adjective

Willing to take risks; bold and venturesome, sometimes without much sense.

It was ***daring*** and foolish for Jerome to walk so close to the edge of the subway platform.

Adverb: **daringly**
Noun: **daring**

The ***daring*** of the acrobats on the high wire was breathtaking.

▶ **derring-do**
noun

A reckless, daring, or careless action.

The pirate's deeds of ***derring-do*** were legendary.

▶ **foolhardy**
adjective

Recklessly careless; unwisely daring.

Andrew wove his motorcycle in and out among the speeding cars; his ***foolhardy*** actions resulted in a bad and nearly fatal accident.

Noun: **foolhardiness**

▶ **hotheaded**
adjective

Quick to anger; quick to act, often without regard to the consequences.

Jerome's ***hotheaded*** response to his girlfriend's dumping him didn't surprise those who had seen his temper before.

Noun: **hotheadness**
Adverb: **hotheadedly**

► **impetuous**
adjective

Impulsive and passionate, sometimes marked by violent force.

Sometimes our *impetuous* decisions can prove foolhardy in the long run.

Adverb: **impetuously**
Noun: **impetuousness**

► **impulsive**
adjective

Inclined to act on impulse rather than on thought; acting without thinking things through.

Impulsive behavior can get us in trouble and cause us to regret our actions.

Adverb: **impulsively**
Noun: **impulse**

► **insolent**
adjective

Bold; arrogant; rude; rash and disrespectful.

The *insolent* student was caught in the act of not only imitating the teacher but also wearing the teacher's coat and hat.

Noun: **insolence**
Adverb: **insolently**

► **madcap**
adjective

Behaving impulsively, madly, or rashly, with little thought or consideration of consequences.

The twins' *madcap* adventure left them stranded 300 miles from home with less than $5 between them.

► **offhanded**
adjective

Performed extemporaneously, without forethought or planning.

Charlie gave such an *offhanded* speech that we were surprised he got a passing grade on it.

Adverb: **offhandedly**
Noun: **offhandedness**

► **perilous**
adjective

Full of or involving peril or great danger.

In the book *The Lord of the Flies* the students from a private boys' school experience many *perilous* adventures when they find themselves alone and without adult supervision after their plane crashes on a deserted island.

Adverb: **perilously**
Noun: **perilousness**

► **rash**
adjective

Characterized by or resulting from ill-considered haste or boldness; reckless.

Never one to make *rash* decisions, my grandfather thought over the situation for a long time before he made up his mind.

Adverb: **rashly**
Noun: **rashness**

▶ reckless
adjective

Indifferent to or disregarding of consequences; careless.

Reckless behavior often leads to remorse and heartache later on.

Adverb: **recklessly**
Noun: **recklessness**

▶ temerity
noun

Reckless disregard for danger or one's own safety; recklessness.

Juana's *temerity* in rushing into traffic to save the runaway kitten made everyone scold her for being so careless about her own safety while praising her for what she did.

Sentence Completion

Circle the word or word pair that best completes the meaning of the sentence.

1. Steven's _____ courage was evident during the tragedy, but Bryan, who lacked such daring, tried to hide his weakness with a swaggering _____.

   A. foolhardy/defiance
   B. insolent/gallantry
   C. dauntless/bravado
   D. steadfast/temerity
   E. tenacious/valiance

2. The frightened kitten held onto the tree limb _____, unwilling to release its grip as its _____ owner climbed a ladder to rescue it.

   A. steadfastly/plucky
   B. gallantly/defiant
   C. dauntlessly/foolhardy
   D. smugly/self-righteous
   E. tenaciously/valiant

3. During her early teens, Alexandra developed such a _____ attitude toward authority that no one wanted to be around her because she was always getting in trouble.

   A. rash
   B. stalwart
   C. defiant
   D. audacious
   E. insolent

4. Despite having had three bouts with cancer, Elsie continued to demonstrate _____; her courage and determination showed her to be (a) _____, unwilling to give up or to give in.

    A. fortitude/virago
    B. tenacity/madcap
    C. insolence/gallant
    D. sanctimony/defiance
    E. complaisance/valiant

5. Lewis and Clark were _____ explorers; even though they were constantly challenged by daunting circumstances, their _____ and resourcefulness kept them going.

    A. steadfast/impetuousness
    B. intrepid/pluck
    C. valiant/insolence
    D. impulsive/tenaciousness
    E. audacious/bravado

Quick Matching

Write the letter of the definition shown in the right column next to the word that matches it in the left column.

_____ 1. insolent   A. bold and dashing

_____ 2. valiant   B. rude and arrogant

_____ 3. gallant   C. unwise and daring

_____ 4. defiant   D. valorous and courageous

_____ 5. foolhardy   E. boldly resistant

Complete the Story

Using these words selected from this unit, fill in the blanks to complete the story.

steadfast	rash
virago	defy
dauntless	valiantly
insolent	audacious
bravado	intrepid
daring	pluck
reckless	madcap
foolhardy	gallantly

Sir Francis Drake _____ led the fleet that defeated the Spanish Armada in 1588. Because of the _____ courage of this seafarer and his _____ ship, the *Golden Hind,* people in England greet one another today with "hello" instead of "ola." Drake truly turned Great Britain into a world power.

If we look beyond the textbook version of Sir Francis Drake, however, we discover that he was a reckless and _____ man who actually displayed more _____ than true _____. In actuality, Drake was an _____ pirate who followed many whims, and whose rude and _____ behavior had greatly displeased Queen Elizabeth I. She could be a real _____ when she became angry. In order to win back her favor, he _____ attacked the entire Spanish fleet for her. With the weather working in his favor, Drake was able to _____ the power of the Spanish Armada, and he won the sea battle in the name of his queen. Some historians scratch their heads and wonder if Drake was truly an

_____ hero or a _____, _____ adventurer, whose _____ and _____ deeds just happened to go the right way.

One Size Does *Not* Fit All

S ometimes the words *small, tiny, large,* or *big* are not precise enough to get the picture across. Below you will find a generous collection of words that have to do with size, amount, or degree of importance. You should be able to find one that's just the right size for your needs. You will find, however, that many of these words are actually descriptors or synonyms for one another. Some are a bit different; others mean basically the same thing.

dearth	minuscule	pittance
diminutive	minute	scant
infinitesimal	mite	scintilla
insignificant	negligible	trifling
Lilliputian	paucity	trivial
meager	petty	

• •

ample	humongous	plethora
behemoth	immeasurable	prodigious
Brobdingnagian	incalculable	statuesque
colossal	infinite	surfeit
copious	mammoth	titanic
gargantuan	monumental	

▶ dearth
noun

A scarcity or lack of supply.

During World War II there was a ***dearth*** of silk available for women's stockings because the military needed the silk for making parachutes.

▶ diminutive
adjective

Very small; tiny. (*Diminutive* is occasionally used as a noun. It refers to anything that is small or the name given to suffixes on words that indicate smallness. For example, the suffix *let* is a diminutive. When it is added to a noun, it indicates a smaller version of that noun, such as a *booklet* or *starlet*.)

Tinkerbell is the ***diminutive*** fairy in the children's story *Peter Pan*.

Adverb: **diminutively**
Noun: **diminutiveness**

▶ infinitesimal
adjective

Immeasurably or incalculably small.

At one time scientists thought they would never be able to study the ***infinitesimal*** nucleus of the atom, but, with advanced technology, this study is commonplace.

Adverb: **infinitesimally**

▶ **insignificant**
adjective

- Of little importance or power.

Everyday, routine, personal problems seem *insignificant* when compared to the problems of drought, famine, or war.

- Small and not important.

After the accident, the dent in the car door was *insignificant* compared to the damage the other car suffered.

Adverb: **insignificantly**
Noun: **insignificance**

▶ **Lilliputian**
noun, adjective

Noun: A very tiny person or thing.

(This word is taken from Jonathan Swift's *Gulliver's Travels*. In this book the *Lilliputians* are very tiny people who live in the land of Lilliput, which is where Gulliver experienced his first adventure.)

When Michael Jordan visits the children's wards in hospitals, he is like a giant among the adoring and appreciative *Lilliputians.*

Adjective:

- Small or trivial in size.

The young couple found a *lilliputian* cottage that suited their needs for a temporary home.

- Not important, petty.

The question was *lilliputian* in light of the seriousness of the situation.

► **meager**
adjective

• Scarce in quantity or extent; in short supply.

After two weeks of rough camping in the hot, humid, mosquito-infested Minnesota Boundary Waters, good humor and food were in *meager* supply while flaring tempers were plentiful.

• Deficient in richness or fertility.

Because the soil was so *meager,* the crops yielded very little harvest.

Adverb: **meagerly**
Noun: **meagerness**

► **minuscule**
(sometimes spelled **miniscule**)
adjective, noun

Adjective: Extremely tiny; very small.

When cooking with hot Thai dragon peppers, the chef must use *miniscule* amounts, or the peppers will overpower all other flavors of the dish being prepared.

Noun:

• Small, ancient, cursive script.

Some of the *minuscules* in the ancient manuscript were so faded that the translators were unable to transcribe the entire text.

• Lowercase letters.

An old-fashioned term for lowercase letters is *minuscule.*

► **minute**
adjective

• Exceptionally small or insignificant.

The hardly visible dent in the car door seemed *minute* to me, but the car's owner was displeased nevertheless.

• Characterized by precise and close scrutiny.

The drill sergeant held a *minute* inspection of the recruits' quarters, looking for a shoe unpolished or blanket not taut.

Adverb: **minutely**

► **mite**
noun

• A very small sum of money.

Widow's mite is a biblical reference to a poor widow whose small donation meant more to her than much larger sums from those who could easily manage to contribute.

• A very small creature or object.

The orphan child was a *mite*—undersized because of her poor care.

The tiny premature infant seemed like a *mite* next to the 9-pound baby in the next crib.

► **negligible**
adjective

Not considered important enough to be worth bothering about; insignificant.

When I receive a *negligible* amount in change from a restaurant bill, I toss the money into the dish by the cash register.

Noun: **negligibility**
Adverb: **negligibly**

► **paucity**
noun

- Smallness of number.

The county officials were disappointed when only a *paucity* of voters turned out for the election.

- Scarcity of amount.

During the drought, there was such a *paucity* of water that the local swimming pools had to close down.

► **petty**
adjective

- Trivial; of little importance.

Because she had much on her mind while planning her wedding, the bride-to-be left the *petty* details to be taken care of by others.

- Narrow-minded; shortsighted.

Sandra was so *petty* that she overlooked the big picture because she was so concerned about trivialities.

- Mean and grudging.

The old woman was so *petty* that she held a grudge for years over some minor insult.

Adverb: **pettily**
Noun: **pettiness**

► **pittance**
noun

A very small amount, often referring to an unusually meager amount of money.

After dropping out of college, the young man could not find employment and had to settle for earning a *pittance* from a job he found working in a kiosk at the mall.

► **scant**
adjective, verb

Adjective: Barely sufficient; falling short of a necessary amount; inadequately supplied.

Because of threatening thunderstorms, only a **scant** crowd gathered for the band concert in the park.

Verb: To shortchange or deal with something inadequately or neglectfully.

Because of her demanding work hours as a lawyer on her way up in the firm, Susan **scanted** on quality time with her children.

Adverb: **scantily**
Noun: **scantiness**

► **scintilla**
noun

A minute amount; barely a suggestion; just an inkling or a spark.

For a brief moment, Carlos had a **scintilla** of hope that he would not get lost in the blizzard.

► **trifling**
adjective

Of trivial or nonsensical importance; not important and easily dismissed.

Heidi's **trifling** plan was so impossible to carry out that everyone dismissed it immediately.

Noun: **trifle**

► **trivial**
adjective

Of little significance or importance; concerned with trivia or inconsequential information; commonplace.

Although the research assignment was supposed to get students to find new and unusual information, Alfred could find only *trivial* facts and unimportant details.

Adverb: **trivially**
Noun: **triviality**

....

► **ample**
adjective

Of a large or great size; fully sufficient, even more than enough.

I remember my grandmother as a large woman with an *ample* lap for me to sit on.

Adverb: **amply**
Noun: **ampleness**

► **behemoth**
noun

Something that is enormous is size and/or power.

The super jet was a *behemoth* flying from Los Angeles to Hong Kong and carrying nearly 300 passengers.

► **Brobdingnagian**
adjective

Immense or enormous. (The word comes from Jonathan Swift's *Gulliver's Travels*. In his second adventure, Gulliver finds himself in Brobdingnag, the land of the giants.)

A giant cherry on an enormous spoon is a famous Minneapolis, Minnesota, sculpture of *Brobdingnagian* proportions.

► **colossal**
adjective

So enormous or gigantic that it seems to defy belief.

Until one actually sees the huge stones at Stonehenge, England, a person cannot appreciate what a *colossal* undertaking it must have been.

Noun: **colossus** (From the *Colossus* of Rhodes, built around 300 B.C., which was a statue of the sun god Helios and was about 100 feet tall.)

► **copious**
adjective

Containing or yielding plenty; bountiful in amount or manner.

Afraid she might miss something in the biology lecture, Arlene not only took *copious* notes, but she also brought her tape recorder to class.

Adverb: **copiously**
Noun: **copiousness**

► **gargantuan**
adjective

Of enormous size, quantity, or volume or capacity.

The grounds of mansion were enormous, and Marty thought he would never get the *gargantuan* lawn mowed and its edges trimmed.

► **humongous**
(sometimes spelled **humungous**)
adjective

Gigantic or extremely oversized.

After the two-hour practice, we were so hungry that the four of us devoured a *humongous* pizza and at least five liters of Pepsi.

► **immeasurable**
adjective

So vast or limitless in size that measurement is not possible.

The young couple felt *immeasurable* love for their newborn baby.

Adverb: **immeasurably**
Noun: **immeasurability**

► **incalculable**
adjective

Impossible or too great to be calculated or resolved.

Because the storm caused *incalculable* damage to the small town, insurance representatives were flown in from everywhere.

Adverb: **incalculably**
Noun: **incalculability**

► **infinite**
adjective

Immeasurably great or large; having no limits or boundaries.

Despite having to deal with a class of 30 squirming, energetic kindergartners, the teacher displayed *infinite* patience.

Noun: **infinity**
Adv: **infinitely**

▶ **mammoth**
noun, adjective

Noun:

• A great, hairy, prehistoric elephantlike creature.

Archeologists discovered the well-preserved remains of a prehistoric *mammoth*.

• Anything of unusual size.

Adjective: Enormous; of great or unusual size or proportions.

Driving the *mammoth* Humvee was a much different experience from driving a Miata.

▶ **monumental**
adjective

• Resembling a monument.

The Egyptian Pharaoh's *monumental* bearing was impressive to his minions.

• Exceptionally large, sturdy, or enduring.

When the teacher assigned the research paper, it seemed like a *monumental* undertaking that I would never be able to complete.

Adverb: **monumentally**

▶ **plethora**
noun

An excessive amount; a surplus.

Because the office assistant thought the boss wanted 12 dozen folders instead of only 12 folders, we had a *plethora* of blue and red folders at our disposal.

► **prodigious**
adjective

• Excessively great in size, force, or content.

The hurricane caused such *prodigious* rain and wind that many houses were severely damaged.

• Exceptionally talented.

Lindsay was such a *prodigious* student that she was in three advanced placement classes, the dance squad, the speech team, and National Honor Society.

Adverb: **prodigiously**
Noun: **prodigiousness**

► **statuesque**
adjective

• Unusually large or outstanding in carriage and/or demeanor.

The *statuesque* news anchor drew everyone's attention—men and women alike.

► **surfeit**
noun, verb

Noun:

• Overindulgence, as in food or drink.

• An excessive amount.

The United States is often looked upon as a country of overindulged people who have a *surfeit* of material goods at their disposal.

Verb: to feed or supply to excess, even to the point of disgust.

Many successful farmers were able to *surfeit* some of their bumper crops to the countries that had been devasted by the hurricane.

▶ **titanic**
adjective

- Of or relating to something awesome or great in size or scope.

In September 1989, Hurricane Hugo was a storm of such *titanic* proportions that large areas of South Carolina were completely devastated by its high winds and torrential rains, at least 26 people died, and parts of the Charleston area landscape were changed forever.

Sentence Completion

Circle the word or word pair that best completes the meaning of the sentence.

1. Some news stations report such _____ information that many viewers consider their stories as _____ and not worth their attention.

   A. diminutive/infinitesimal
   B. insignificant/trivial
   C. minute/petty
   D. ample/trifling
   C. meager/incalculable

2. Because of ideal weather conditions last year, Iowa had a _____ of corn, so the state was able to export some of its harvest.

   A. dearth
   B. paucity
   C. monument
   D. surfeit
   E. scintilla

3. The information Sandy found in the reference book was so _____ that she didn't even bother to take any notes.

   A. diminutive
   B. petty
   C. immeasurable
   D. scant
   E. incalculable

4. In the next reference, however, Sandy discovered a
   _____ of information, so she took _____ notes
   on her topic.

   A. ampleness/minute
   B. dearth/incalculable
   C. paucity/immeasurable
   D. mammoth/surfeit
   E. plethora/copious

5. Despite some _____ complaints among the 300
   passengers, the _____ overseas jet made good time
   between New York and London.

   A. petty/colossal
   B. paucity/monumental
   C. modicum/statuesque
   D. scintilla/prodigious
   E. infinitesimal/ample

Quick Matching

*Write the letter of the definition shown in the right column next
to the word that matches it in the left column.*

_____1. pittance   A. fully sufficient; more than
                              enough

_____2. ample   B. suggestive of a monument

_____3. Brobdingnagian   C. little money

_____4. statuesque   D. incalculably small

_____5. infinitesimal   E. immense or enormous

Complete the Story

Using these words from this unit, fill in the blanks to complete the story.

infinite	prodigious
colossal	gargantuan
copious	incalculable
plethora	diminutive
minute	monumental
scintilla	minuscule
immeasurable	humongous
insignificant	

From its often _____ depths and the _____
number of creatures living in the water or on its beaches, the
ocean provides us with a _____ of contrasting sizes.
_____ starfish may be no bigger than the nail on your
little finger, but other starfish species can be the size of an
extra-large pizza. _____ humpback whales dine on
_____ amounts of _____, nearly invisible
plankton. Humpback infants, however, could never be called
_____ newborns. These youngsters weigh in at a
_____ 1500-2000 lb at birth! _____ coral reefs are
also living creatures within the ocean. They are slow-growing,
however, showing barely a _____ of change during the
course of a year. The variety of fish species living in the
oceans and seas is _____. The smallest nurse shark may
be a scant 10 inches long, and the infamous great white
shark, whose _____ strength and menace were made
famous by the movie *Jaws*. Finally, we cannot overlook the
crab. The most _____ of this species is the soldier crab,

measuring a mere 15 millimeters, while the _____ giant crab can measure over 400 millimeters. Creatures great and small can be found in the ocean.

Review 3

These sentences include words from the previous five sections

Sentence Completion

Circle the word pair that best completes the meaning of the sentence.

1. The poor, struggling college student found that his scholarship money gave him only a _____ to live on, so he had to find a job in order to have enough food.

   A. pittance
   B. immeasurability
   C. surfeit
   D. mammoth
   E. scintilla

2. Even though the generous congressman had been _____ in his support of the arts and charities, the press did not hesitate to _____ him when his name was linked to a local scandal in his home state.

   A. admirable/eulogize
   B. penurious/disparage
   C. laudable/extol
   D. selfless/abominate
   E. magnanimous/excoriate

3. The performer became so impressed with herself that her
_____ attitude caused her fans to dislike her for her
_____ behavior.

A. frugal/audacious
B. reproachful/creditable
C. haughty/reprehensible
D. egocentric/estimable
E. admonitory/reckless

4. The crystal figurine was _____, despite the
_____ value that the insurance company had placed
upon it.

A. infinitesimal/meager
B. diminutive/colossal
C. copious/infinite
D. incalculable/insignificant
E. a pittance/negligible

5. Although Louis was _____ and fun to be around, his
high spirits often led to _____ behavior that
sometimes got him in trouble.

A. audacious/priggish
B. convivial/impetuous
C. admiral/selfless
D. intrepid/deplorable
E. amiable/creditable

6. Pamela is a quiet girl whose _____ is often mistaken for _____ by people who don't make the effort to get to know her.

A. reticence/aloofness
B. steadfastness/parsimony
C. geniality/insolence
D. tenacity/providence
E. self-righteousness/altruism

7. Bruce had always been a poor loser, so when the referee called a foul, instead of reacting in a sportsmanlike, _____ manner, he let his _____ nature provoke him into arguing with the referee.

A. openhanded/deplorable
B. gallant/smug
C. penurious/madcap
D. laudable/hotheaded
E. benevolent/resolute

ANSWERS

1-A, 2-E, 3-C, 4-B, 5-B, 6-A, 7-D.

Index

Essential SAT words have **bold** locators.

FINAL WORDS

No, this is not another list of vocabulary words to study. If you've spent time learning the vocabulary words in this book and going over the exercises, you are well on your way to conquering the SAT. Don't forget to prepare for the other sections of the exam as well, by brushing up on your math and refreshing your writing skills. The SAT expects you to do it all. With lots of effort and some good fortune as well, I am sure you will succeed. Good luck!

Denise Pivarnik-Nova